BEYOND SPECIAL NEEDS

Susan Hart taught for 16 years in secondary and primary schools. She spent two years as a researcher in primary schools and initial teacher training; and has for the past six years been involved in in-service education with experienced teachers. She has published many articles on special needs support and collaborative teaching and learning. With Denis Mongon, she is the co-author of *Improving Classroom Behaviour* (1989, Cassell).

BEYOND SPECIAL NEEDS

ENHANCING CHILDREN'S LEARNING THROUGH INNOVATIVE THINKING

Susan Hart

Paul Chapman
Publishing Ltd

Paul Chapman Publishing Ltd
144 Liverpool Road
London N1 1LA

British Library Cataloguing in Publication Data

Hart, Susan
Beyond special needs : enhancing children's learning
through innovative thinking
1. Special education
I. Title
ISBN 1 85396 301 1

Typeset by Anneset, Weston super Mare.
Printed and bound in Great Britain.

A B C D E F G H 9 8 7 6

Contents

Acknowledgements

I am indebted to many teachers and children for their contribution to the ideas explored in this book, and particularly to the following:

- the teachers and children in the school where I carried out my research, who made me so welcome in their classroom and allowed me to observe and participate in their collective experience;
- Dr. Mike Oliver, for supervising the research in a subtle and sensitive way;
- colleagues and students, past and present, with whom I have worked at the University of Cambridge Institute of Education, whose experience and insight has enriched, challenged and helped me to clarify my own thinking: and especially, Mel Ainscow, Maggie Balshaw, Mary Jane Drummond, Marion Dadds, Jennifer Nias, Martyn Rouse and Judy Sebba;
- colleagues from the London Borough of Enfield Language and Curriculum Access service and Educational Psychology service: Neil Parr, Penny Travers, Randa Price, and Jeanette Redding, who brought their own perspectives to bear on the ideas in a most helpful and constructive way at a critical point in the writing;
- Tony Booth, who provided a sounding board for the ideas on a number of occasions, and with whom conversations have always been fruitful;
- Tish Crotty, for helpful and perceptive comments on the manuscript at draft stage;
- Pauline Hanson, for help in the preparation of the manuscript;
- Richard Winter, whose interest in ideas, education and learning has enabled him to be both a support and inspiration.

Susan Hart
January 1996

Introduction

Emily looks up at me, her face tense, worried, unsmiling. I ask her to choose a book to read with me and she frowns. She says that she is no good at reading and suggests politely that I might try someone else. She is just six years old.

Barry is just starting secondary school. In our conversations, he is knowledgeable, articulate, humorous, self-mocking. Yet when he starts to read a simple text, he stumbles and stops over almost every word.

Jamie, aged thirteen, is cocky, streetwise, one of the gang. In private, he weeps with embarrassment and frustration at his inability to read and write, yet refuses point blank to take advantage of any individual support offered. He prefers to sacrifice learning to read, it seems, rather than lose face with his friends by being seen to require extra help.

Christine, fifteen, serves out her time in school as if it were a custodial sentence. She declares herself 'useless' and a 'dunce' at all aspects of school work. Yet, outside school, she cooks, shops and looks after the home for working parents, and takes considerable responsibility for the care of a younger brother with cerebral palsy. On work experience placement in a residential home for elderly people, she is commended for the quality of her work and for the sensitivity with which she builds relationships with residents. If human sympathy and interpersonal skill were valued by schools as a measure of ability and achievement, Christine would have been a high flyer.

These young people and countless others whom I have encountered over the years provided the impetus for the development of the ideas presented in this book. They convinced me that there are many questions about children's learning for which we do not as yet have satisfactory answers, and made me determined to keep searching for ways of making the experience of school learning a more rewarding and life-enhancing one for more children. I hope that readers will recognize in these accounts similarities with young people that they have come into contact with, worried about and tried to encourage into further effort in the course of their work as educators. This book is intended for teachers whose professional experience and aspirations for children's learning have led them, as have mine, to be dissatisfied with currently available ways of thinking about and pursuing concerns about children's learning and who are actively seeking alternative ways forward.

I have called the book *Beyond Special Needs* because I believe that in order to open up new possibilities we can and should now set aside once and for all the language of 'learning difficulties' and 'special needs'. This language shapes and constrains our thinking, limiting our sense of the scope available to us for positive intervention to a narrowly circumscribed set of possibilities. It has discouraged mainstream teachers from using their knowledge, expertise and experience as fully and powerfully as they might in pursuing concerns about children's learning. The experience of the past two decades has drawn attention to enormous scope *within* mainstream education for enhancing learning and achievement amongst those whose development gives cause for concern. Although much effort has been invested in pursuing this scope, and some headway certainly made, I believe that we have barely begun to recognize and realize the possibilities. At least part of the reason for this is because the language of learning difficulties and special needs keeps recreating the idea that something *additional* to or *different* from what is generally available to all within mainstream education is needed in order for some children to learn more successfully.

The book sets out to propose, justify and illustrate by example an alternative way of thinking about and pursuing concerns about children's learning which focuses upon and exploits more fully this mainstream potential. This approach enables teachers to follow up concerns about specific children without individualizing the 'problem', or disconnecting it from the social processes which have produced it as a cause for concern. Indeed, by making those connections visible, it seeks to restore mainstream teachers' belief in their own power to take positive action in response to concerns about children's learning. In this way, I believe we will become able to tap into a vast reservoir of mainstream professional knowledge, expertise and creativity which for too long has been under-used. Although the book aims to heighten awareness of the scope and expertise that exists within *mainstream* schools for addressing concerns which were previously referred to special education, I believe that the approach proposed is relevant to *any* school context, mainstream or 'special', where teachers are seeking to understand children's responses to the experience of school learning in order to foster and enhance individuals' learning and development.

Whilst the approach could form the basis for schools' formal response to the Code of Practice (DfE, 1994) as will be discussed in Chapter 7, it is first and foremost intended to be used by teachers working individually and on their own initiative. It is not conditional upon the availability of additional support or resources, although additional support time (appropriately used) would certainly strengthen and extend what an individual teacher can achieve alone. Nor does it expect teachers to possess superhuman capacities or assume an exhaustive knowledge of literature and research. What the approach does depend upon is a spirit of open-mindedness and willingness to entertain alternative possibilities. It depends upon the conviction that the picture we currently have of children's characteristics as people, and their abilities as learners is susceptible to change; indeed, that we have the power and means to bring about changes ourselves by thinking in ways that continually open up new possibilities. I call this 'innovative thinking'.

The approach involves going to work on our *existing* understandings of a situation – or child's learning – that is causing concern, in the belief and expectation that, if we do so, we will be able to discover *new* ways forward, even in most seemingly intractable situations. We do this by asking ourselves questions that help to free up our thinking in order to become able to see new possibilities. The book is about this process, and how I came to realize its potential for pursuing concerns about children's learning as a result of a classroom research study (Hart, 1994). Although this research is the direct and immediate source of the ideas presented, these ideas also draw extensively upon the whole of my previous teaching experience. It is necessary, therefore, to explain briefly the links between the various different professional pathways along which attempts to understand learning and literacy difficulties had taken me prior to embarking on the research which forms the basis for this book.

TEACHING BACKGROUND

For the first eight years of my teaching career, I taught French in an inner city secondary school. There was much debate at that time about whether or not children who were struggling with literacy should be given the opportunity to learn a foreign language. I was uncomfortable with the argument, put forward by some modern linguists, that 'less able' and 'slow learning' children would never learn enough to make the time spent worthwhile, and so would be better off spending the time on boosting their weak literacy skills (Hornsey, 1972). It seemed to me that we were in no position to dismiss children's potential for language learning, when we had not yet seen what they *could* achieve if learning materials and teaching approaches were developed that were appropriate, motivating and capable of offering the chance of positive achievement to all children.

I was also attracted by the argument that, apart from any gains in the target language itself, having the opportunity to learn a modern language could present a critical turning point for children who had already come to see themselves as not very successful learners. It was the one area of the curriculum where differences of prior attainment were of lesser significance, and where facility with literacy in English was not a prerequisite for success. A breakthrough in this one area might then have a positive effect on children's self-perception and approach to learning more generally.

I wanted to pursue this idea and see for myself if learning French could achieve this effect in practice, before coming to a conclusion about what might be the best course of action in the interests of children. After eight years, which did indeed yield some encouraging evidence that learning French could play such a role for some children, I decided that I wanted to concentrate on working with those children who were least successful at school in conventional academic terms. I re-trained as a teacher of language and literacy and took up a new post as a remedial teacher in another inner city secondary school. I worked initially on a withdrawal basis, and the small group situation allowed me to gain much closer knowledge of children whose struggles with school learning – and with literacy acquisition in particular – had led them virtually to abandon hope that any success would come from further effort.

It was during this time that I began to realize just how much scope there actually is for enhancing these children's learning within mainstream classrooms which for all sorts of complex reasons remains unexploited and often, seemingly, undetected. Children would arrive for their reading lessons seeking help with worksheets and textbooks which they could not hope to read independently. They would present me with homework tasks which they had no idea how to begin. I began to realize that there was not just a literacy gap but a lack of genuine connection between the substance of school learning and these children's purposes, interests and concerns. I became dissatisfied with trying to teach literacy on the margins of the curriculum, when there was so much potential for positive development within mainstream contexts. I began to seek out mainstream colleagues who were prepared to work with me collaboratively, so that we could explore together ways of enhancing children's opportunities for learning and their literacy development through subject teaching.

Like many other schools at the time, we gradually moved towards a more integrated system of support. Rather than simply adding support to an existing curriculum, we began to focus on ideas for developing the general curriculum to try to make it more interesting and accessible to all. Approaching the task of providing support for children experiencing difficulties in this way seemed to present many advantages in principle: avoiding the need to single them out for special treatment and enabling the ideas developed to support their learning to be introduced to the potential benefit of all children (Hart, 1986a, 1986b, 1989a).

However, this shift of emphasis was by no means unequivocally welcomed, either in my own or in other contexts. Hard-pressed subject teachers protested that they could not take on any more. The presence of a support teacher raising questions about provision for particular children could be both personally uncomfortable and professionally undermining. I found that most of the possibilities that occurred to me could not be pursued either because of time constraints or for fear that raising them would seem to be implying criticism of colleagues' work.

After six years, I decided to move into support work in the primary sector. I thought that perhaps collaborative forms of support stood more chance of success in a primary context where teaching was not so fragmented and each individual teacher had responsibility for one group of children only. I wanted to know more about what happened in the early years of education, and explore what further might be done to enhance learning before all the inhibitions and defences that complicate the task at secondary age have hardened into an almost impermeable resistance to school learning. I was fortunate to work on a team which placed us full time in a school for two terms. This way of working allowed for relationships to develop and possibilities for experiment to open up that would not readily be available to peripatetic support teachers.

Nevertheless, I found many of the same obstacles to the development of more collaborative forms of support work at primary level as I had encountered at secondary level. I began to feel that the precious resources that were being spent on me, as a support teacher, were actually inhibiting the kinds of developments that I now believed would *most* benefit children referred to me for support. Mainstream teachers looked to me for support; yet the kinds of support I was in a position to offer were not those that I now thought would be most helpful to children or teachers in the long-term.

Instead of investing scarce resources in the provision of additional adult support for individual children, I was now convinced that available resources would be better spent on providing time and opportunity for mainstream teachers to explore possibilities for enhancing learning and achievement that they could introduce themselves. But where did this leave my work as a support teacher? Was I arguing myself out of a job? By a lucky coincidence a job came up to research the work of support teachers, which allowed me time in addition to pursue a project of my own. I decided to take time out from teaching in order to stand back and take a fresh look at these problems.

RESEARCH STUDY

At the time, then, when I carried out the research study which forms the basis for this book, I was not currently working as a support teacher but as a full-time researcher (on a temporary basis), with one day a week allowed to work on my own study. I decided to use my study to help me come to terms with the frustrations that I was currently experiencing in my support work and to help me to make a decision about my own future professional role. In spite of my conviction that mainstream developments should be the main priority, I thought that there might still be a legitimate role for support teachers for a number of reasons which I wanted to explore further.

A more detailed account of the background to the research, the selection of the particular setting and how the research itself was carried out will be provided in Chapter 2. Briefly, for the purposes of this summary, I looked for a situation where teachers had already introduced, on their own initiative, a significant development in some aspect of practice that I thought would help to make the learning environment more supportive for all children. I found a Year 5–6 primary classroom where teachers had recently introduced a 'process' approach to the teaching of writing (Graves, 1983; Calkins, 1983, 1986) which had been in my mind as a potential area for development since reading about the research some time before.

This research seemed to be suggesting that many of the learning problems, reluctance and resistance to writing that I tried to remedy in my work as a support teacher might no longer occur if (as Graves and his colleagues propose) children were given more control over the process and content of their writing, if they had a genuine audience for their writing and teaching was genuinely tailored to their individual purposes and concerns. Finding a situation where such conditions were already in place and appeared to be working well would put me in a position to find out the extent to which these theories were actually borne out in practice and review the implications for the continued need for additional support.

At the beginning of the study, I did not imagine that anything could occur during the course of the research that would change my conviction about where the principal focus needed to be placed in pursuing concerns about children's learning. My conviction about the need to put the main emphasis upon supporting general developments within mainstream teaching was so firmly rooted in and confirmed by my experience that it did not seem open to question. What I hoped that the research would do was to help me to reach a new understanding of what part *additional adult support* might constructively have to play alongside and in conjunction with this wider conception of *support through curriculum development*.

However, for reasons which will become clearer as the story of the research unfolds, the research did bring about a fundamental shift in my perception of the central task itself. It shifted my attention from a particular view of what might most equitably and constructively be *done* to support children's learning, to the *thinking that generates our ideas* about what might be done in response to concerns about children's learning. I realized that the ways of thinking associated with the language of learning difficulties and special needs lead us to ask certain kinds of questions at the expense of others. It is these other kinds of questions that need to be asked if we are to open up and exploit more fully than before the scope that exists for enhancing learning within mainstream schools and classrooms. I concluded that we need to establish an alternative way of thinking about and pursuing concerns about children's learning, cast in a different language, if we are to become able to open up these wider possibilities.

These conclusions offered new insight into the reasons why we had run into so many difficulties in trying to develop more collaborative, cross-curricular approaches to support. As long as we were still using the language of learning difficulties and special needs to make the case for working in this way, it was difficult to redirect attention to possibilities within mainstream teaching without at the same time reflecting negatively upon teachers' existing practice. In order to explain why it was not sufficient simply to add on additional support to existing provision, we tried to widen explanations of learning difficulties and special needs to show that mainstream learning environments could create or contribute to the difficulties experienced by children. Many teachers were prepared to accept this analysis and work to adjust and improve their teaching, but it was not an empowering message. For others, it led to a reassertion of contributory factors outside of the school, over which teachers, however conscientious and skilled, can have little control.

The study enabled me to appreciate that what was hindering further progress was not teachers' resistance to change, or unwillingness to accept that existing practice might be a contributory factor in children's difficulties. It was to do with the way that the case itself was being made. The way that we were trying to bring mainstream teaching into the equation was not just strategically unhelpful, it was also flawed in principle. The research made me realize that many possibilities for enhancing children's learning and achievements would be overlooked if we were to limit our sights only to those areas of practice thought to be contributing to difficulties or susceptible to improvement.

My close study of two children's learning over a period of several months convinced me of the need for a much more sophisticated analysis of the scope for enhancing learning that exists in any school or classroom: an analysis which is far more respectful of the complexity of the teacher's task and recognizes the key role that the teacher's existing knowledge, experience and expertise must play in its discovery and realization.

The dynamics of teaching and learning are so complex, that any learning situation is rich in potential for yielding new insights that suggest new possibilities for practice. The ability to probe those dynamics and generate new, soundly based ideas about what might be done to enhance children's learning is an expression of expertise, not something to be undertaken only if existing practice is considered to be in need of improvement. We need to keep our attention focused on mainstream practices, not because these might turn out to be the *source of difficulties*, but because our knowledge of the dynamics of teaching and learning is our principal *source of insight* into *possibilities* that might be tried in response to concerns about children's learning. To look elsewhere for solutions is to disconnect ourselves from our main source of power to make a difference to children's learning.

OVERVIEW

The process of reflective analysis which I call 'innovative thinking' is designed to support teachers in pursuing concerns about children's learning by seeking out that potential. My overall aim in this book is to make a convincing case for pursuing the task in this way, and to explain what the approach entails in sufficient detail for readers to be able to see immediately how they might apply it in their own work. The structure of the book reflects this aim.

In Chapter 1, I introduce the approach itself and explain how it took shape as a result of my attempts to come to terms with difficulties encountered in the course of my research, and work through their implications for practice. I examine the knowledge and expertise which the approach requires, and show that it makes use of the same resources which teachers bring every day to the complex task of classroom teaching.

In the next section, I present the two detailed studies of children's learning which were the immediate source of the ideas presented in this book. These illustrate the new insights that were opened up for me, as a result of probing the dynamics of each child's engagement with the particular learning opportunities provided. They show how these insights could, in a situation where I had a direct teaching responsibility, have been translated into new ideas for supporting and enhancing children's learning, as well as informing my thinking and practice generally. The studies are not intended to replicate practice, since clearly no teacher is routinely able to observe and reflect upon individual children's learning in such a sustained and uninterrupted way as I was able to do in the course of my research. The studies provide the detail that will allow me to bring the ideas in the book to life, and illustrate and develop them in a concrete way.

Chapter 2 provides the necessary context for understanding the two stories and, in particular, the purposes for which the studies were originally undertaken. I explain why an initiative in the teaching and learning of writing was chosen as the focus for the research, the particular features of the workshop approach that I imagined would be supportive of children's writing development and how I set the research up to discover their impact on children's learning in practice.

In fact, the task of making sense of these children's learning, and reaching conclusions about how progress was bound up with the particular learning opportunities provided, turned out to be far more problematic than I had anticipated. The two accounts of children's learning both start from an examination of the kinds of difficulties experienced in each case. They show how the process of resolving them led to new understanding that was relevant not just to these children's learning, but to my thinking about teaching, learning, assessment and writing development generally.

Chapter 3 explains the uncertainties encountered in attempting to make sense of the progress made by one child, Annette, over a period of two terms. I explain how the study led me to probe more closely into the patterns identified in her development by exploring what might count as progress from her point of view. I explore how the choices she made and purposes she pursued appeared to be bound up with the specific features of the writing workshop, and examine the new questions and possibilities for further supporting and enhancing her learning that were opened up through this analysis.

Chapter 4 explains the challenges presented by a second child, Adrian, who drew my attention to the limitations of the understandings and vocabularies that I had available for conceptualizing and describing children's writing development. Before I could describe Adrian's progress and explore how it was bound up with the learning opportunities provided, I first had to learn, through extended observation and discussion with him, how to put into words what was significant about his writing.

In the third section of the book, I draw on the content of the two stories to illustrate and explain the basis for the ideas presented in the first part of the book. In Chapter 5, I explain what led me to change my perception of the central task. I explore the basis for the claim that, because the dynamics of teaching and learning are so complex, any situation is always rich in potential for yielding new insights and understandings in which to ground new ideas for supporting and enhancing children's learning. I look at the insights and new possibilities opened up in the case of the two children I studied, and examine the potential for using the study of individual children's learning as a source of ideas that can inform our work to the benefit of all children.

In Chapter 6, I explain how the research led me to the view that there can be many different, yet legitimate, readings of the same situation or child's learning, depending upon the particular aspects we choose to focus on and the particular resources which we bring to bear to help us to make sense of what is happening. The task is not to discover the one 'true' account of a child's learning, but to establish criteria that allow us to have confidence in using a particular reading to inform our teaching. I examine the basis upon which I felt able to have confidence in my two accounts, for the purposes of the research, even though I was also convinced that other legitimate stories could have been written, and draw out the parallels for pursuing concerns about children's learning in practice.

In the final part of the book, I move the discussion beyond the context of this particular research to consider the wider context of current and future developments. In Chapter 7, I summarize the main themes of the approach presented in this book and contrast it with other ways of thinking about and pursuing concerns about children's learning. I explain why I am confident that the style of analysis illustrated in the case studies can be scaled down to a form that can be managed within the constraints of normal teaching, and consider what contribution the ideas in the book might make to the development of school policy. I suggest that the requirements of the Code of Practice (DfE, 1994) could be met via an approach based on innovative thinking, and examine what the implications might be for the staged assessment process and for the use of targeted resources.

Finally, in Chapter 8, I consider the implications of the study for the development of practitioner research. I suggest that the knowledge and expertise needed for innovative thinking are powerful resources which can also be used for the purposes of classroom research. I explain how I used the research in part to explore the idea that practitioners do not necessarily need to acquire additional knowledge of research methods and skill in applying research techniques; rather they need opportunities to use and develop the analytic expertise *already acquired* through teaching. I make a case for opportunities to be made available for teachers to contribute to the development of our collective understanding of the dynamics of learning and teaching. I argue that the study of individual children whose learning gives cause for concern can play a central part in this process. I also look at the contribution which innovative thinking – in the context of practice or research – could potentially make to the development of education generally, and suggest that this approach could make a major contribution to raising achievement for all children.

1

Introducing Innovative Thinking

'Innovative thinking' is a way of *generating new ideas* about what might be done in response to concerns about children's learning. It involves probing more closely into the dynamics at work in a particular situation, in the belief and expectation that, if we do so, we can always find ways of positively influencing and changing a situation that is causing concern – or our perception of it – through the use of our existing resources. It is based on the principle that, because the dynamics of teaching and learning are so complex, any situation is always capable of yielding new insights that will suggest new ideas for practice, if we think in a way that opens up new possibilities.

The framework which supports innovative thinking operates through the use of five questioning 'moves', each of which opens up a different perspective on the situation that the others leave unexamined. These moves will, I believe, be familiar to teachers as strategies which they already use in making sense of what is happening in their classroom and deciding how to respond. When the five moves work together, however, they create a powerful tool for helping teachers to move forward with a problem that has not previously responded to their efforts to address it at a more intuitive level. They are a means of *transforming* concerns about children's learning into new understandings which suggest new possibilities for supporting and enhancing their learning that were previously inaccessible to us.

The approach can be used at an *individual* level, to help teachers find new ways forward to support the learning of individual children who have not responded as well as they would wish to previous efforts to help. It can also be used at a more general level to pursue more *generalized* concerns about, say, truancy or behaviour or literacy development which involve many children and might be addressed, at least in part, through a common strategy. In this book, I am concentrating mostly upon its application to individual children, because in my experience, teachers' most urgent and immediate concerns usually relate to specific children. However, I will use my two studies of individual children to show how the two levels connect up, and to demonstrate that *both* can open up insights and possibilities of potential benefit to *all* children.

In this first chapter, my aim is to outline the framework which supports this process of reflective analysis, and explain how the idea of innovative thinking took shape through my attempts to come to terms with problems encountered in the course of my research. I will examine the links between the five questioning moves and the thinking teachers do in the course of ordinary teaching, and show how the approach makes use of the same knowledge and expertise which teachers bring every day to the complex task of classroom teaching.

THE EVOLUTION OF THE FRAMEWORK

At the beginning of my research study, I imagined that having the luxury of more or less unlimited time to explore the meanings of children's classroom responses would allow me to feel more confident in the conclusions that I reached than was usually the case in the course of my normal work. In fact the opposite happened. Having the time to sit back and think, in someone else's classroom, without the constant pressure to rush to conclusions, heightened my awareness of the complexities and uncertainties that beset the task of making sense of children's learning and deciding the most appropriate and constructive response.

I became increasingly aware of the many different, often conflicting interpretations that could be made of the same evidence; indeed, it seemed that every interpretation I came up with was open to question from another point of view. I started thinking about the consequences of these uncertainties, in practice, for children. It was clear that different interpretations would suggest different ways of responding or lines of further enquiry to support the child's learning. Which interpretation was settled upon therefore mattered considerably, since it would have important consequences for learning opportunities subsequently made available for the child.

Initially, I thought that what was needed was to establish a sound basis for deciding between interpretations. Gradually, though, I began to see that there was a more important lesson to be learnt. These differing interpretations came about as a result of probing the meaning of the situation from different points of view. Each of these points of view was important because each opened up a different perspective upon the situation. What was needed was not to establish a sound basis for deciding between interpretations, but to ensure that whatever judgements were arrived at had taken into account all these different points of view.

These different perspectives are reflected in the five 'questioning moves' which make up the framework for innovative thinking. I began to see the potential for using this framework as a way of pursuing concerns about children's learning when I realized that the kinds of questioning that ensure a sound basis for judgement *also* provide the means of moving thinking on. The process of opening up taken-for-granted elements of an *existing* interpretation is the means by which we become able to see new possibilities. It is the means by which we move beyond our existing understandings and transform our concerns into new, soundly based strategies for supporting and enhancing children's learning in practice.

The five questioning moves

The discovery of the five questioning moves began during the course of my observations of one child, Annette, when I found myself continually fluctuating between what I saw initially as 'positive' and 'negative' readings of her activity and behaviour. If a 'negative' interpretation occurred to me first, this would quickly be counteracted by a positive alternative reading of the same material, or vice versa. For example, in my early observations, I noted that she spent most of her time 'drawing an elaborate picture and talking to her friend'. Writing was produced, it seemed, only after considerable coaxing from the teacher and required constant support.

The initial impression which I formed of her, based on these observations, was of someone who, for reasons I did not yet understand, was 'reluctant to write'. Assuming that this reluctance was a response to a particular situation, my first reaction was to begin speculating very tentatively about how it might be linked to features of the learning environment. Was sufficient support and stimulus being provided for writing? Was the opportunity to work collaboratively in this case perhaps more of a distraction than a positive resource?

Then, alongside these thoughts, a completely different reading of the situation would present itself. Perhaps what I was seeing was not 'reluctance to write' at all but someone for whom drawing, rather than writing was still the central medium of expression at this stage of her development. What was I assuming children ought to be doing during the lesson, against which I was defining Annette's response as 'reluctance'? Where did these norms come from, and did they stand up under scrutiny? Perhaps the proportion of drawing, talking and writing which Annette was establishing for herself was quite legitimate and balanced, in view of the considerable struggle which she had to endure to put her ideas into writing. What writer does write uninterruptedly? What writer does not engage in diversionary tactics? Would I be able to sustain concentration on writing, surrounded by thirty others, at a time not selected by myself?

Thus, the positive readings seemed to emerge in response to the negative readings, as if to say: 'Hold on a moment, let's consider this from another angle. This 'negative' reading depends upon a set of norms and assumptions which merit closer examination. It would be quite possible to come up with an alternative interpretation in which the child's response is not seen as problematic at all'. A similar process happened in the opposite direction, when a positive view of Annette's response on a particular occasion, or her learning over time, would be challenged by an alternative, less positive reading.

Initially, I took this to be a healthy sign of an exploratory research process, assuming that the basis for deciding between interpretations would eventually become clear. Gradually, however, I began to realize that if I was Annette's teacher, what would best serve her interests would be not to find some satisfactory basis to choose between my positive and negative perspectives on her learning, but to ensure that my initial perception of her 'reluctance to write' had been examined from both points of view. The differing interpetations came about as a result of probing the meaning of Annette's responses, and my perceptions of her responses in different ways:

- *Making connections:* This form of probing takes the perception of the child's behaviour (Annette's 'reluctance' to write) in the terms in which it is expressed, and tries to pursue its meaning as a response to the learning environment. It tries to see how the child's response is bound up with features of school and classroom experience and in what ways these might be susceptible to influence by the teacher.
- *Contradicting:* This form of probing helps us to see the underlying norms and assumptions which lead us to perceive a child's response as problematic in some way ('Annette is reluctant to write'), by offering a legimate alternative reading of the same situation (e.g. 'this is a perfectly appropriate balance between drawing, talk and writing for a child at Annette's stage of development').

Relating this to practice, I could see that, if I was teaching Annette, I would need to be probing my perception of her seeming 'reluctance to write' from both angles, otherwise my understanding of her learning would leave important aspects of the situation unexamined, and a whole dimension of possibilities unexplored. For example, the 'concern' as expressed contained an implicit norm about how children *ought* to spend their time during writing workshop sessions, and what balance between rehearsal, relaxation and intensive bouts of writing might be seen as acceptable. It assumed that children ought to be able to write to order, and in a sustained way rather than in short bursts, interspersed by talk. All of these assumptions might usefully be re-examined. On becoming conscious of them, I might be led to revise them and, by implication, to revise my perception of the child's activity as deficient.

On the other hand, if we reconstruct Annette's 'reluctance to write' as a perfectly legitimate response, then this may be taken as evidence that learning conditions currently provided are supporting her learning effectively. How long then should we wait for her to make the transition from drawing to writing? How do we know that she would not have engaged much more enthusiastically and committedly in writing if some action had been taken (for her individually or for the whole group) to stimulate enthusiasm and interest in what to write about? Limiting ourselves to questioning norms and assumptions might, on its own, lead us to opt for non-intervention when there might be much that could be done to stimulate and support the child's learning more effectively.

The two moves thus provide a vital counter-check for one another because they each open up a feature of the situation that the other takes for granted. Asking questions of the first kind, without counterbalancing these with the second, could be unhelpful (and even damaging) if it leads us to try and change a situation that does not need changing, or where the problems that initially concerned us were a reflection of the limitations of our own understanding rather than that of the child. On the other hand, if our questions were limited to those of the second kind, this could lead us to settle for a strategy of non-intervention when there was much that we could do to support and stimulate Annette's writing further.

The child's eye view

Two further moves came to light as a result of considering the perspectives underlying the different interpretations I found myself making in my observations of Annette's learning. One I call 'taking a child's eye view' because it involves the teacher in stepping outside her own frame of reference and trying to reconstruct the meaning of the situation from the child's perspective. Why should Annette be choosing to respond in a way which I interpret as 'reluctance to write'? Had she perhaps set up for herself a nice, cosy little situation which would enable her to get through the lesson as painlessly as possible? Was she creating a situation where little was expected of her, and then basking in the warmth and encouragement of her teachers for any little effort she did make? Was this a gendered response which teachers should avoid colluding with? Or was Annette's commitment to her drawing a reflection of genuinely significant, personally meaningful activity which I was perceiving as an easy option only because of my inability to step outside my own frame of reference and appreciate what might count as significant from the child's point of view?

This third way of probing our thinking about children's classroom responses challenges and complements the other two. It suggests connections with the context which might not otherwise be made, because it explores the gap between the teacher's intentions and ideas of 'good practice' and how learning activities and opportunities are re-interpreted and experienced by the child. It offers alternative ways of interpreting a child's activity, capable of countering negative perceptions, by trying to appreciate the activity as a product of active intelligence and making the imaginative leap required to understand its logic and significance from a child's perspective. It therefore opens up possibilities for understanding and intervention on the part of teachers which might otherwise be overlooked.

Although it can, and should, involve seeking the child's own account as an important source of information, there is a difference between seeking children's views and taking these into account and the shift of perspective proposed by this questioning move. As the work, for instance, of Donaldson (1978), Pye (1988), Armstrong (1981, 1990), Drummond (1993) and Easen (1987) illustrates, the language and constructs of our analysis remain those of adults not children, and offer an interpretation that children themselves would not be in a position to articulate.

The impact of feelings

A fourth interpretive move involves considering the impact of feelings upon our interpretations of children's learning. It examines the part that our own feelings are playing in the meanings that we construct in relation to a particular situation. It invites us to stop and ask ourselves to what extent our

Ready-made interpretations provide the *raw material* for generating new possibilities

- Initial interpretation of child's response which triggers concern and desire to intervene in some way to facilitate learning:

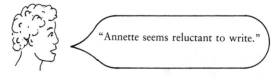

"Annette seems reluctant to write."

- "Maybe her friend is distracting her from working."

↓

- "Or maybe this is a sign that the environment needs to provide more support and stimulus for writing."   (Making connections)

↓

- "Not necessarily. A preference for drawing could be a perfectly legitimate response at this stage of development, providing a necessary support for writing."   (Contradicting)

↓

- "Yes. Her absorption with drawing could be a sign that the activity has genuine significance for her."   (Taking a child's eye view)

↓

- "On the other hand, it could also be a convenient avoidance strategy, to avoid doing what she finds difficult and challenging."   (Contradicting via a child's eye view)

↓

- "By helping Annette with her spelling, maybe I am colluding with her view of herself as someone who can't spell."   (Making connections)

↓

- "Perhaps I have a vested interest in seeing her learning in negative terms because it is the beginning of the research."   (Noting the impact of feelings)

↓

- "I've only met Annette a few times, so I do not have enough to go on yet, to have confidence in any particular reading of the situation. I will wait and see how things develop."   (Suspending judgement)

Figure 1.1   An exploratory conversation

interpretations are a projection of our own desires and fears, and what new insights we can gain by acknowledging this dimension. I was aware, for example, as time went on, of an impulse to look for a positive construction that could be placed on classroom events, and screen out my more negative perceptions of Annette's learning because of my personal investment in the ideas that were, in a sense, being put to the test through my study. I *wanted* to see evidence of progress because I hoped and expected this to occur. I *wanted* to present her learning in a positive light because the version of myself as a teacher that I wanted to see reflected in my judgements was of someone with the personal regard and mental flexibility to appreciate children's endeavours to learn rather than deprecating their weaknesses. Moreover, as I finished the first complete draft of Annette's story, it occurred to me that the account which I had finally come up with was one which could also be applied to my own learning. What I had written was not simply an account of Annette's development, but also, in important respects, of my own.

We may feel we ought to leave our own problems at the school gate, but in practice feelings may be the most powerful of all determining factors in what possibilities we see and what possibilities we consistently rule out or overlook. The impact of our feelings may lead us to see or treat seriously only the negative meanings and ignore the positive ones. If we are feeling generally well, optimistic, confident in ourselves personally and professionally, then this will affect both our perceptions of what is a matter for concern and our sense of optimism and belief in our ability to respond positively to it. Conversely, if a more negative sense of ourselves and our prospects prevails, we may find it difficult to see positive interpretations and may feel powerless to take initiatives to influence and change the situation.

My conclusion, then, was that we could be confident in the sound basis of our judgements if these had been reached through a process which had subjected our thinking to examination from *all four points of view*. An interpretation reached via the use of any of the forms of questioning individually, however insightful, could only ever offer a partial perspective. The use of each kind of questioning ensured that all the dimensions of the interpretive context that needed to be taken into account had indeed been taken into account. The interplay *between* them ensured that insights emerging via the use of a particular mode were automatically questioned and re-examined from other perspectives. The account, in the end, should represent a synthesis of insights arising from all the moves working in combination.

Suspending judgement

Finally, I realized the need for a fifth type of questioning as a result of the problems encountered in my study of a second child, Adrian. From the outset, I had a sense that the available evidence of Adrian's writing abilities concealed as much as it revealed about his knowledge, understanding and skills, and that therefore more information was needed before I could feel confident in making any judgement relating to these. As time went on, I also became increasingly aware that I did not have the knowledge to do justice to the understandings which he demonstrated in the compositional aspects of his writing. The most appropriate response seemed to be to acknowledge the limitations of my resources, and take steps to develop these . This meant suspending judgement for the time being in order to allow Adrian to teach me, through our conversations and through the reading that I was conducting alongside, a language with which to describe the qualities I appreciated in his writing.

This fifth move involves a conscious decision to stand back from the interpretive task, while pursuing various different lines of enquiry suggested by the understandings and evidence so far available. It complements and challenges the other interpretive moves because it reminds us that our existing resources necessarily limit what we 'see' and the understandings that we can reach through the application of our existing knowledge and expertise. It reminds us not to jump too soon to conclusions that are not warranted by the information available, to remain open to the possibility that the child's response is highlighting some feature of the situation as yet unknown or inaccessible to us. In some situations, the best that we can do in the interests of the child, is to wait, listen, watch closely and learn more: to learn from studying the child what we need to know to be able to support his or her learning.

Thus, in Adrian's case, as in Annette's, my strategy was to think about what the consequences would be in practice for children, if certain features of the situation that had a bearing on my interpretations were to remain unexamined. This helped me to establish the range of questions that would need to be thought about if I were to have confidence that any new understandings reached did provide a sound basis for action. If we base our professional responses upon interpretations which neglect one or more of these perspectives, then we will be leaving crucial aspects of the situation unexamined and hence possibilities for supporting and enhancing the child's learning unexplored. On the other hand, if we do make use of all five modes in combination, we have available a powerful means of generating new ideas about what we can further do to support the child's learning. To summarize, the different interpretive moves are as follows:

- Making connections: This move involves exploring how the specific characteristics of the child's response might be linked to features of the school and classroom learning environment. We ask ourselves: 'What contextual influences might have a bearing on the child's response?'
- Contradicting: This move involves teasing out the underlying norms and assumptions that lead us to perceive the child's response as problematic. It asks: 'How else might this response be understood?' It seeks to uncover the norms and assumptions underlying a judgement, so that these can be reviewed and evaluated.
- Taking a child's eye view: This move involves trying to enter the child's frame of reference and see the meaning and logic of the child's response

from the child's perspective. It asks: 'What meaning and purpose does this activity have for the child?'
- Noting the impact of feelings: This move involves examining the part that our own feelings are playing in the meaning we bestow on the situation, and in leading us to arrive at a particular interpretation. It asks: 'How do I feel about this?' and 'What do these feelings tell me about what is going on here?'
- Suspending judgement: This move involves recognizing that we may lack information or resources to have confidence in our judgements, and therefore holding back from making judgements about the child's needs while we take steps to acquire further resources.

This framework is not intended to be followed in a rigid and prescriptive way. It maps out the thinking processes that we have available to use and shows how they can be used progressively and systematically to help move forward with a concern and see new possibilities where previously it seemed that we had reached the limits of our available resources. I believe that teachers can and will use them flexibly, just as they do routinely in their everyday teaching as they monitor children's responses and probe their meanings in order to decide on appropriate action.

LINKS WITH TEACHERS' CLASSROOM EXPERTISE

Although innovative thinking no doubt sounds complicated when it is put into words like this, I would argue that it is no more complicated than the thinking-on-their-feet that teachers have to do every day as they process simultaneously the multiple sources of information which inform them of what is happening in their classroom, and respond expertly to that information in order to maintain a productive and pleasant working atmosphere. Indeed, I believe that the five kinds of questioning I have identified will be familiar to teachers as questions which they ask themselves in the course of their normal teaching. All that is new about the framework is the way that it uses these questions *together* as a tool for probing more rigorously and systematically the dynamics of a situation causing concern and helping teachers to move forward with a problem that has not previously responded to their efforts to address it at a more intuitive level.

Trying to make connections, for instance, is what we do all the time as we continuously monitor what is going on in our classrooms and make adjustments in the light of the feedback provided by children. If children seem restless or inattentive, for instance, we automatically review a repertoire of possibilities, to help and decide what we can do to influence it. Do we need some more air in? Do the seating arrangements need altering? Is it something to do with the way we have presented the task, with the materials selected, with the language we have used? Is it the time of day, week or term, and if so would it be better to try another approach? In a split second, we make our reading, decide what tack we will take and make the corresponding adjustments. We then use the children's responses as further feedback, and if necessary begin the process again. When a child's learning gives cause for concern we can use the same knowledge and skills to help us open up new insights into the influences that are shaping the child's response. The only difference is that, in this case, we think through the possibilities more consciously, systematically and rigorously than in other situations. We not only review possible connections with what is going on in the immediate situation, but also try to understand the child's response in its inter-relationships with all dimensions of school experience, which we know has a bearing on children's learning, and which we may be in a position to influence.

It is also part of our expertise as teachers to be able, in a split second, to counter one reading of a situation with one or more others as a way of helping ourselves decide how best to respond. For instance, I might be feeling irritated by a group of pupils in the back row who seem to have taken no notice of my request for attention. This is an interpretation based on the evidence that they did not look up, put their pens down, stop work, which I am implicitly invoking as criteria for 'appropriate behaviour' in response to a request for attention. I *assume* that the pupils know this and therefore they have knowingly infringed norms of appropriate behaviour. Then, just before I leap in and speak to them smartly, it occurs to me that their behaviour might mean that they did not hear my request, or they might indeed be listening, and know that they are, but not showing it through their non-verbal behaviour (and perhaps because they are anxious to finish the work). The element of doubt prompts me to remove the edge of irritation and reprimand from my voice when I address them directly to check that they are listening, and so avoids introducing tension unnecessarily into the situation.

Schon (1983) refers to this ability to entertain, at any given time, more than one interpretation of classroom events as 'double vision'. The ability to see more than one possibility is a reflection of expertise, not a sign of inexperience, inadequacy or indecision. When we are concerned about a child's learning for some reason, we can bring that same skill, and the resources upon which it depends, to bear on the evidence that is causing us concern, and use it to help us explore alternative possibilities. As a result of attempting to 'see differently', we may rethink our norms or gain a new perspective on the evidence such that we change our perception on what we thought was the problem.

It is also, I believe, a familiar move for teachers to take to try to put ourselves in the child's shoes and appreciate the logic and meaning of their responses from their perspective. Many teachers look beyond misbehaviour and inattention, to see if fear of failure or lack of understanding may lie behind. Teachers recognize that children are active agents in the complex dynamics of schooling; they have their own agendas which they pursue at least as energetically as the agendas that we try to negotiate with them. These are not necessarily easy to appreciate from an adult's point of view. We try to be alert to the possibility that what at first glance appears to be a misunderstanding or a wrong answer may, on closer inspection, turn out to be an ingenious but *different* understanding from the one that we were expecting or anticipating. To gain insight into children's thinking, many teachers ask children to verbalize their thoughts or show their working on paper so that they can appreciate the intelligence as well as the flaws in the thinking that led to a 'wrong' answer. They can then convey appreciation and build on that intelligent thinking in their response to the child. This way of thinking corresponds with teachers' aspiration to achieve genuinely child-centred teaching.

I imagine, too, that most teachers will not have difficulty in recognizing that their perceptions of pupils' learning and behaviour are indeed shaped by how they are feeling on a particular day and also by the qualities of their on-going relationship with a particular child or class. Behaviour that invites humorous repartee on Monday morning may be interpreted as a serious challenge to authority by the time that we are tired and stressed on Friday afternoon. Poor quality work from a class or child that we like and get on well with may more readily prompt a sympathetic response than with a class we have a less positive relationship with. In this case, 'poor quality' work may seem indicative of pupils' lack of commitment and effort with their work. Since we are only human, we recognize these differences and notice, for instance, when pressure of work leads us to an explosion that is out of all proportion to the perceived offence. We take trouble to try to correct imbalances that we are aware of in our treatment and perceptions of pupils.

Even suspending judgement, because we recognize that we lack adequate information or resources, is a strategy which will be familiar to teachers, in spite of its seeming impracticality in the busy world of school and classroom. Teachers in my experience are very anxious to keep an open mind about children, particularly on first meeting, and to avoid them becoming locked into fixed identities from which it is difficult to escape. In the early days of working with a new group of children, they are anxious not to prejudge children based on their prior achievements and records. They want to allow children scope to negotiate their identities and relationships afresh. Many teachers try to teach in a way which is genuinely open-ended, in the sense of allowing children to teach us what help they need in order to learn, rather than assuming that we can select the expertise ready-made from our existing repertoire. The ability to teach in this way, in my view, is not an abdication of responsibility but a reflection of genuine respect for learners and for the seriousness of their individual endeavours to cope and learn in school.

Moreover, innovative thinking not only makes use of the same *expertise* but also the same *knowledge* which teachers bring every day to the complex task of classroom teaching. All experienced teachers have extensive knowledge about the dynamics of teaching and learning and what makes a difference to how children behave and how well they learn in school. We draw on this knowledge constantly, both consciously and intuitively, in planning lessons, in interpreting what is happening minute-by-minute in classrooms and in reviewing what happened in order to plan future lessons.

The knowledge comes partly from contact with the ideas of others, through professional training and through reading. Much is learnt, too, from observing other teachers and talking to colleagues. However, by far the greatest part comes from experience. Through everyday contact with children in classrooms, and the continual processing of classroom happenings, we build up an understanding of the different aspects of school and classroom life which have bearing on how children respond to our teaching and help to determine the extent and limits of their achievements. Amongst those which spring immediately to mind are, for instance, the impact of relationships with staff and peers, the content of what is taught, how it is presented, the range of learning opportunities provided, classroom language, teachers' expectations of children, use of praise, rewards and feedback on work, seating arrangements, systems used to group children, the management and timing of activities, contact with parents and links with the cultural and linguistic communities served by the school. Our own personalities, backgrounds, preferences, beliefs, judgements and responses to individual children also play a central part in these dynamics.

I believe that this reservoir of professional knowledge, together with the expertise required to process and respond to what is happening minute-by-minute in our classrooms, is our most powerful and, as yet, under-used resource for pursuing concerns about children's learning. The five questioning moves which make up the framework for innovative thinking are the means by which we marshall our existing knowledge of what makes a difference to generate ideas about what might be done, here and now, to make a difference with respect to a particular situation or child's learning that is giving cause for concern.

My argument, then, is that the framework of questioning moves which supports the process of innovative thinking does not involve knowledge or expertise beyond that which teachers already use in the context of their ordinary work. Innovative thinking is a means by which teachers can use their *existing* knowledge, understanding and expertise to generate *new* insights, understandings and previously unthought of possibilities for practice. Of course, other people's ideas also have a part to play in extending, enriching and challenging ideas that individual teachers can generate themselves. Our individual thinking powers can be greatly strengthened and enriched by continuing contact with the ideas of others, either directly through discussion with colleagues, or indirectly through published research and literature. We are never *dependent*, though, upon external input in order to to discover new possibilities.

Once we are convinced of the importance of asking these questions of our own thinking, and have recognized the power which asking them gives us, I believe that it is possible to make use of them to respond to concerns about children's learning in the context of ordinary classroom teaching. The process can also be slowed down and used more consciously and deliberately as the situation demands. Situations of practice do not often allow for slow and careful deliberation of all the possibilities on the spot. But once we have a grasp of the different dimensions of the interpretive context which need to be taken into account, we can ensure that, over time, we submit our under-standings of children's learning to examination via all the different perspec-tives. If our actions based on a preceding analysis do not produce the outcome that we were hoping for, we have a way of reviewing the original analysis and considering possibilities that maybe were not considered, or were ruled out, in the first instance.

As I shall illustrate in more detail later, the kinds of insights which emerge through this process do not necessarily imply a lot of extra work for teach-ers. Many of the possibilities which are opened up are ones which can eas-ily be incorporated into ordinary classroom teaching without making dramatic changes or needing further resources or undertaking general cur-riculum development work. Some of these will be specific to the teacher's work and approach with the particular child, some the teacher will find can be incorporated into work with the whole class, and potentially to the ben-efit of everyone.

A major worry for mainstream teachers is always that they will neglect the needs of other children if they put any more time and energy into pur-suing concerns about children's learning. Through the case studies and sub-sequent discussion, I will try to show that the time spent on innovative thinking is not necessarily time denied to other children. If we pursue con-cerns about children's learning through innovative thinking – whether focused upon individuals or conducted at a more generalized level – the analysis will help to raise questions and open up new insights, understand-ings and possibilities for the development of practice which can positively influence and enhance the achievements of all children. Innovative thinking, I shall try to show, can be a continual stimulus to the development of edu-cation generally.

2

Towards a More Supportive Curriculum

So far, I have introduced the main themes of the approach presented in this book and begun to explain how this evolved from my studies of two children's writing development. Here, I present these two stories in full, so that I can use them to illustrate, justify and develop in a more concrete way the ideas presented so far in the remainder of the book. First, though, it is important to explain the context in which these studies were originally undertaken, and the purposes that I had in mind in embarking on the research. In particular, I need to offer some background to the initiative in the teaching and learning of writing which I chose to study, and the specific features of the approach that I thought would be supportive of children's writing development. This will help to clarify what I was hoping to learn through studying these children's learning, and also to explain the *changes* in my overall thinking brought about through the research and which led to the approach presented here.

BACKGROUND TO THE RESEARCH

During the years that I worked as a remedial teacher and a support teacher, I had gradually become dissatisfied with the whole idea of pursuing concerns about children's learning by providing support in the form of 'additional adult help for identified individuals', whether this support was offered in the classroom or through withdrawal. I realized that providing support in this way prevented all sorts of *other*, richer and more integral opportunities for enhancing children's learning within the mainstream curriculum from being discovered or pursued. I began to develop a view of 'support' focused on these alternative possibilities: using additional resources to develop a more supportive curriculum. The aim would be to enhance learning opportunities provided within the general curriculum, with particular emphasis on those that were likely to be especially beneficial for children experiencing difficulties.

It seemed to me, for example, that if we could bring about a shift in the overall *balance* of learning opportunities provided across the curriculum, this could significantly increase and enhance children's engagement with the tasks of school learning. The balance was heavily weighted towards reading and writing, towards individual work rather than group work, towards teacher-initiated activities rather than pupil-initiated work, towards closed tasks rather than open-ended, investigative learning. I thought that if we could only shift that balance in the other direction and make these other opportunities more routinely available within the mainstream curriculum, this would really make a difference to children with limited literacy. It could also be justified in terms of widening the range of learning opportunities available to all children.

I could see tremendous scope, too, for combining support for children's literacy development with support for their subject learning by exploiting more fully and more productively opportunities for using texts as a source of information and instruction in subject areas. I wanted to explore how small group discussion could be used to support more active and sustained engagement with texts, and help to create a more generally supportive climate for learning. The literature of the period reflects a similar orientation, increasingly redirecting attention to possibilities for developing more supportive curriculum, not simply at classroom level, but at the level of overall school organization, policy and practice (e.g. Bell and Best, 1986; Booth, Potts and Swann, 1987; Ainscow and Tweddle 1988; Clough, 1988; Thomas and Feiler, 1988; Dyson, 1990).

However, I had had only limited opportunities to pursue such developments in practice and discover the extent to which they would help to create a more supportive learning environment (Hart, 1989a). I also had a number of unresolved questions in my mind about the continued need for additional adult support, which I wanted to use the research as an opportunity to think through. Although my experience had convinced me that additional resources for supporting children's learning should first and foremost be used to foster developments within mainstream teaching, I was doubtful about the idea of dispensing altogether with additional adult support for children experiencing difficulties. I wanted to be sure that a dogmatic or single-minded focus on general curriculum development within the mainstream did not lead me to overlook *other* possibilities for supporting children's learning that were not necessarily applicable to everyone. No amount of general review and development of the curriculum, for instance, would overcome the difficulties created for a child with an undetected hearing loss, which could continue to affect his or her learning until it was recognized and appropriate action taken. There was also the whole controversial area of dyslexia, and its implications for the provision to be made for children, to which I wanted to give further thought.

Giving priority to development work aimed at creating a more supportive curriculum did not necessarily rule out the provision of other sorts of individual support as well. The problem was how to define and organize this so that it did not detract from, or become a substitute for, the wider task. Through the research, I hoped to come up with a new understanding of the relationship between the two modes of support that would help me to decide how best to develop my own future professional work.

Investigating a process approach to writing

I decided that what I needed to do to help me think about these unresolved questions was to find a situation in which some sort of initiative of the kind I had been envisaging had already become the established way of working for a particular group of children. In such a situation, I would be able to discover if the developments that I thought would be supportive actually did seem to have the sort of positive impact on children's learning that I had imagined. This would then provide a specific context for re-thinking the place of additional support for individuals alongside wider developments.

In theory, any of the ideas for enhancing learning opportunities through the curriculum that had been taking shape in my mind through experience, in-service training and reading over a number of years could have provided an appropriate focus for the study. The initiative I chose was selected, as is often the case, partly on the basis of the range of opportunities that were actually available to me. Some years previously I had read about research carried out in the United States (Graves, 1983, 1984; Calkins, 1983, 1986; Willinsky, 1990) which had offered new insights into the processes of learning to write and convincing recommendations about what might be done to create conditions that were more supportive of children's writing development generally. The central theme of this research is that conditions need to be created that will enable children to find their own voice and take control of their own learning.

> The child's marks say, 'I am.' 'No, you aren't,' say most school approaches to the teaching of writing. We ignore the child's urge to show what he knows. We underestimate the urge because of a lack of understanding of the writing process and what children do in order to control it. Instead, we take the control away from children and place unnecessary blocks in the way of their intentions. Then we say 'They don't want to write. How can we motivate them?'
>
> (Graves, 1983, p. 3)

In order to enable children to exercise control, the workshop approach is organized in a way that encourages children to make (or help one another to make) their own independent decisions at every stage of the writing process. Most importantly, children are encouraged to write from personal experience about topics that are personally important to them. Offering freedom of topic choice is the means of tapping into their inner urge to write:

> Children's voices push them ahead. Voice is centred in a vision and has a faint image of the achieved mountain top, the piece completed in victory . . . Schools forget the source of power in children's writing. The school experience can cut down egos or remove voice from the writing, and the person from the print, until there is no driving force left in the selection. We then hear the familiar questions, 'How can we motivate them into writing? How can we get them to write?'
>
> (Graves, 1983, p. 244).

To help children choose topics that are important to them, the research recommends that teachers should build up 'territories of information' about each child, that is knowledge about the child's cultural and experiential world, activities, expertise and interests outside of school. Children can also help one another in this, and indeed can often do so more successfully than the teacher:

> The best confirmation comes from children who note what other children know. This is one of the critical elements within the studio-craft atmosphere, so desirable in supporting learning and the writing process. Children extend far beyond what teachers can do in helping each other establish their territories of information.
>
> (ibid., p. 23)

The positive use of the resources of the whole group to support and enhance one another's learning is a key feature of the approach. Children are encouraged and in some cases specifically shown how to help one another for a whole variety of purposes in the process of writing. They help one another choose topics, explore and check spellings, discuss ways of expressing ideas, ask one another questions which help to decide what to write, read one another's writing to give feedback and ask questions, and so on. Calkins (1983, pp. 19–20) explains the function of collaboration as follows:

> For me, it is helpful to think of writing as a process of dialogue between the writer and the emerging text. We focus in to write, then pull back to ask questions of our text. We ask the same questions over and over again, and we ask them whether we are writing a poem or an expository essay. . . . In my research, I have found that when teachers ask these questions of children in conferences, children internalise them and ask them of each other in peer conferences. Eventually, they ask them of themselves during writing.

Interaction with others, both with the teacher and with other children, is an essential part of the process of learning to write, and the classroom has to be organized to support and facilitate this. The idea of creating a genuine audience for children's writing, which has been a central theme in debates on the teaching and learning of writing since the mid 1970s, is also built into the approach, with children providing the audience for one another's writing, being encouraged to treat one another's work as seriously as they do the books of published authors, and indeed to make their own 'published' books to read in the classroom:

> Publication is important for all children. It is not the privilege of the classroom élite, the future literary scholars. Rather it is an important mode of literary enfranchisement for each child in the classroom. And it may be that children who have space–time problems, with little audience sense, benefit even more from the publishing step.
>
> (Graves, 1983, p. 55)

To summarize, the workshop approach encourages children to exercise control by making choices at each stage of the writing process: not just about what to write but whether to write alone or with others, what materials to use, how often to redraft, when a piece of writing is finished or has outlived its interest, which pieces to publish, and so on. The teacher does not abdicate responsibility for guiding this process. Once children have taken con-

trol and learnt to use one another as a resource, the teacher's main task is
to go round and work with individual children on their writing as it is happening. Instead of marking and commenting on work after it is written,
teaching can take place in the midst of the process and while the children
are making the decisions that they may benefit from the teacher's help with.
At all stages, the teacher tries to ask questions about the writing that will
maintain the children in control and allow them to reveal and determine
what help they need from the teacher to achieve their intentions.

Links with my own thinking

These key principles underlying the workshop approach to writing development linked up with my own ideas about what might be done to make the
curriculum more supportive of children's learning in a number of ways. The
theme of 'control' struck a chord because I had often experienced, in my
own work with children, a sense that they had given up on themselves, that
they had completely lost control of their ability to learn and their belief in
their own competence as learners. When reading aloud, children would often
stumble on with a text, saying nonsense words yet making no attempt to
correct these unless they were pointed out by the teacher. There were many
children who would not try to spell an unknown word or get on with a task
on their own; they would wait, as if helpless, for the teacher to come and
help with the spelling or show them how to tackle a task. An approach
which specifically set out to enable children to exercise control over their
own learning was therefore a very appealing one. If control had already been
lost, would children be able to regain it, simply by offering them the opportunity? How would we know unless we tried?

The idea that children's *individual* learning might be enhanced by making
more creative and productive use of the resources of the *whole group* was
one which had been central to my own thinking for a number of years, and
which I had begun to explore myself through my own mainstream teaching.
As well as the social and cognitive benefits that might come from increased
opportunities for collaboration, I was interested in the potential for creating
more time through this means for the teacher to spend sustained, quality
time with individuals or groups, helping them with their writing. Lack of
time is the perpetual cry of all teachers. It seemed to me that if only we
could create styles of classroom management which allowed children to operate independently of the teacher for extended periods, then we might create
more time for quality interactions between teachers and individuals.

The approach also seemed to have the potential to bridge the gap which
I had so often perceived between children's own relevances and concerns and
the substance of the school curriculum. By actively encouraging children to
choose their own topics and write directly from personal experience, the
'workshop' approach seemed to offer the means for making children's out-
of-school knowledge and interests central rather than peripheral to curriculum concerns, and so perhaps would be able to enlist greater commitment
on the part of children to the task of learning to write in school.

I was interested, too, in how children would respond to the change of authority relationship between teachers and learners implied by the principle that, with this approach, *everyone* in the classroom is both a teacher and a learner. It suggested a radically different social climate which might in turn have a significant impact on learning. It also seemed to be a way of giving concrete expression to the value placed on the resources of every child in the group, a way of ensuring that every child's uniqueness was acknowledged and listened to. The teacher's learning stance demonstrates respect for what is important to children, a willingness to listen and an openness to the unexpected. Such an approach could significantly change the social dynamics operating within the classroom, in ways that could be beneficial to those who previously had not experienced a sense that they had much to contribute to the work of the group.

Finally, the principle that teachers should also regard themselves as learners in their interactions with children fitted with my own conviction regarding the need to keep searching for ways to enhance learning opportunities for all children within the general curriculum. Graves (1984, p. 193) emphasized that his work was intended to provide a resource to support teachers' own thinking about children's writing, not a new orthodoxy that teachers should take on ready-made as a substitute for their previous ways of working.

> The exciting thing about having the children teach us and having us teach ourselves in our own writing is that teaching becomes a process of discovery in its own right. Orthodoxies continually make us use old data, without today's fresh evidence. Orthodoxies make us tell old stories about children at the expense of the new stories that children are telling us today.

For all these reasons, then, a classroom where children's writing development was organized along these lines seemed to offer precisely the opportunity that I was looking for. If it was indeed the case that children's learning could be significantly enhanced by creating an environment based on these principles, then we should be putting our efforts into helping establish such conditions and into supporting the implementation of the approach rather than simply offering additional individual support for those experiencing most difficulty within existing arrangements.

The class

As part of a series of classroom visits carried out when I first took up my full-time research post, I came across a class of nine- to eleven-year-olds in an inner city primary school, where the teachers had already introduced, and seemed to have established successfully, a workshop approach to the teaching and learning of writing closely based on this research. I was greatly impressed by the industry and independence showed by the children in their workshop sessions. One of the teachers responsible for this class (whom I shall call Karen) was an ex-advisory teacher for literacy and had introduced the approach into the school (where she was now deputy head) the previous year. By now, most of the teachers were organizing the teaching of writing in this way. Karen timetabled herself to support them as often as she could, and ran workshops for staff outside school hours for teachers to share ideas and problems together. She already had considerable experience herself of working in this way, and was clear about what she was trying to achieve with the children and why. She and the class teacher seemed to have a good relationship with one another and with the children. Between them, they seemed to be able to win the willing co-operation of most of the children most of the time.

There were many other features of the way that teaching and learning were organized that appealed to my current understanding of 'good practice': the quality of relationships between teachers and children, the positive, work-oriented atmosphere which the teachers seemed to have managed to create, the care and attentiveness with which the teachers engaged with the learning of individual children, the expectations of success and praise that were discerningly offered to all. This classroom came closer to my current image of an ideal learning environment than any I had ever created myself or previously participated in. Studying children's learning in this context would be a way of moving beyond a set of imagined possibilities to an appreciation of how supportive these ideas actually were in practice, and what continuing place there might be for additional adult support alongside broader mainstream developments.

In this situation, I would be able to observe individual children learning to write and see if the features of the approach that had appealed when I first read the research did indeed seem to foster learning in the way that the research suggested. How, for example, would they respond to the opportunity to choose their own topics, establish their own territories of information, publish their own work? Would they flounder or flourish? How would they make use of opportunities for collaboration and did this appear to be significant in the way that I had supposed? What kind of help did the teacher provide, and how was this related to their progress? What kind of written work did they produce and how did this develop over time? How did their development appear to be related to the way in which they chose to respond to the particular range of learning opportunities provided? What evidence was there of any difficulties, what appeared to be the source of these, and how did features of the workshop approach help (or otherwise) in overcoming them?

RESEARCH PROCEDURE

I visited the class once and sometimes twice a week for a year, during the time that was specifically set aside for personal writing. I observed and increasingly joined in with what was going on, but without slipping into the role of teacher. I chose two individuals to study in depth, and another five or six to follow in a less detailed way in order to explore the significance of differences emerging within the group. The boy and girl chosen for detailed observation were selected on the basis that their writing, at the commencement of the study, showed characteristics in common with the writing of children who used to be referred to me for extra help in my work as a support teacher.

I made notes of what each of the children did during the course of the session, what attention they received from the teachers and the work which they produced. This included both observation and discussion with the children individually, and observation of their involvement in group or whole-class sharing and teaching sessions. I also kept a record of the writing which they produced, including drafts and odd pieces of paper on which spellings were tried out. As far as possible, I annotated the writing with information drawn from observation and discussion (the talk that accompanied each stage of the writing, points at which teacher help was sought or offered, spontaneous comments which the children made to me about their writing, or about anything else, and my own responses to them, periods when writing was sustained or interrupted, and the circumstances which appeared to be associated with these different patterns of work).

My aim was to document each child's progress over the period of the study and try to relate these findings to the features of the writing workshop approach that I had imagined would be particularly supportive of children's learning. I also planned to document any difficulties that arose, in order eventually to reconsider the significance of these for the support teacher's role. Clearly there was no scope here for a 'before–after' comparison, since I had no direct knowledge of these children's work prior to the introduction of the process approach. I also doubted the value of research which sought to make such comparisons since classroom processes are so complex that it is difficult to isolate a particular aspect and prove that it has made a difference. My approach was a more qualitative one, more akin to the kinds of judgements that teachers would be in a position to make when evaluating such initiatives in the context of ordinary practice. I took my lead from an example in the work of Calkins (1983), one of Graves' associates, who presented two samples of writing by a boy called Craig (pp. 106–7), one produced at the beginning and one at the end of the year. The contrast between them was strikingly dramatic. Frustratingly, though, no insight was provided in this instance into the processes through which this change had been brought about and how it had been supported by the learning opportunities provided. My aim was to try to gain insight into these processes, for each of the children studied, and document the path of their development over the period of the study.

THE CASE STUDY 'STORIES'

However, my attempts to identify progress ran into unexpected difficulties. The case study 'stories' in the next two chapters start out from these difficulties and document the evolution of my thinking as I attempted to resolve them and reach an understanding of how the path of each child's development was bound up with the particular features of the writing workshop. I follow the ideas arising through to their implications for practice, even though I had no teaching responsibility for these children, because I wanted to explore the implications of these practical outcomes for the future of support work.

Even when I had eventually arrived at accounts which I felt confident could be defended as legitimate and justified readings of the evidence, I was also well aware that there were other versions of each child's story that I *could* have written, with equal claims to legitimacy, if I had I chosen to pursue differently the various possibilities opened up for me by the evidence. For example, I did not pursue gender as a specific lens through which to read and interpret the significance of the children's activities or the content of their writing, even though I was aware of this as a possible route for further enquiry. I was aware, too, for reasons that I will explain later, that I would have made different sense of the material if I had carried out the study a few years earlier or later, when I would have had different experience and resources to bring to bear on classroom evidence. Other people, too, would have made different sense of the same material as they drew on their own personal reservoir of knowledge, experience and understandings.

No doubt, as you read the two stories, you will also find yourself disagreeing in places with my interpretation of the children's writing, or perhaps even overall. If so, then I hope it will not deter you from reading on. The research made me realize, in a way that was far from obvious before, that people will inevitably 'read' classroom events and the significance of developments in children's learning differently, even those who have close and detailed knowledge of the situation. Therefore, the insights that they derive from their reflection will also necessarily be different.

The question is not to determine the one correct reading, but to establish that whatever insights are generated from the evidence are *soundly based*, so that we can have confidence in using hypotheses derived from them to guide the development of practice. The stories illustrate the new insight that, on this occasion, given a particular set of purposes, this classroom and these two children yielded for me. Nevertheless, the situation also had the potential to yield many *other* new insights, for me or for others, which could have suggested other possibilities for the development of practice. Any classroom contains virtually limitless scope for yielding new insights and understandings. That is the principle which underpins the approach presented in this book, and which I shall elaborate in more detail in the second section of this book.

3

A 'Person without Turf'? Annette's Story

Those children for whom it is most difficult to come up with a territory of information are those who need it most. They are often the children who find it difficult to choose topics, to locate a territory of their own. They perceive themselves as non-knowers, persons without turf, with no place to stand.

(Graves, 1983, p. 24)

My attention was drawn to Annette during my earlier visits to this class-room, because there was something about her thin, frail appearance and seemingly listless demeanour which was more than a little reminiscent of many children I had worked with in my time as a support teacher. She seemed prepared to commit words to paper only if there was an adult on hand to help her with spellings. Her constant plea was 'I don't know how to spell it!'. When an adult was not there to work with her on a one-to-one basis, Annette seemed to be quite content to carry on drawing and talking to her friend, Angie, who came to join her for writing workshop sessions from a parallel class.

I decided to choose Annette as one of my children for in-depth study since my initial impressions of her dependence upon adult support suggested that she would pose quite a challenge to ideas for creating a supportive envi-ronment that were based on the principle of children exercising control over their own learning. I observed her activities in a sustained way from November to April of that school year, until she suddenly left at the end of the Spring term. She had mentioned the possibility on a number of occa-sions during the preceding weeks, but her teachers had heard nothing from her parents and so assumed that this was not a serious intention. Annette's earlier explanation had been that she was unhappy at the school because the other girls picked on her. I had seen some evidence of friction in her rela-tionships with other children, and indeed came to see this as playing a sig-nificant role in the evolution of her learning during the period I observed her.

During this period, some quite remarkable changes certainly did occur. However, I also had some reservations about the path which her develop-ment seemed to be taking. To explain this, I shall compare two instances of her writing activity – one recorded at the beginning and one from near the end of the study – and examine the differences between them. On the first occasion when I observed her activities in a sustained way, she spent most

23

of the session (as I noted in Chapter 1) doing an elaborate drawing and talking to her friend. After some coaxing from her teacher, she agreed to add some writing to her drawing, but stopped constantly as she wrote claiming that she did not know how to spell the words. She eventually produced three sentences of writing, positioned at the margins of the page (see Figure 3.1). On the later occasion (which, unexpectedly, turned out to be our penultimate meeting), of her own accord she came to sit beside me to do her work.

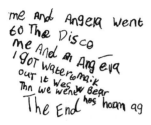

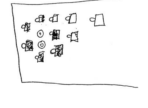

Figure 3.1

Without any prior discussion, she produced a page of writing fluently and effortlessly, stopping only to ask for help with two spellings (see Figure 3.2).

If we compare the writing produced on the two occasions, a number of changes can be noted in the later piece which might be taken as indicative of significant progress. In the second piece of writing, pictures have given way to writing as the central medium of expression. The quantity of writing has increased dramatically, and its presentation is now more conventional, filling the page across and down. Annette has now achieved standard spelling for most of the words used. Her independent attempts (not shown here) to spell less familiar words ('brhtday' and 'holrday'), showed that she

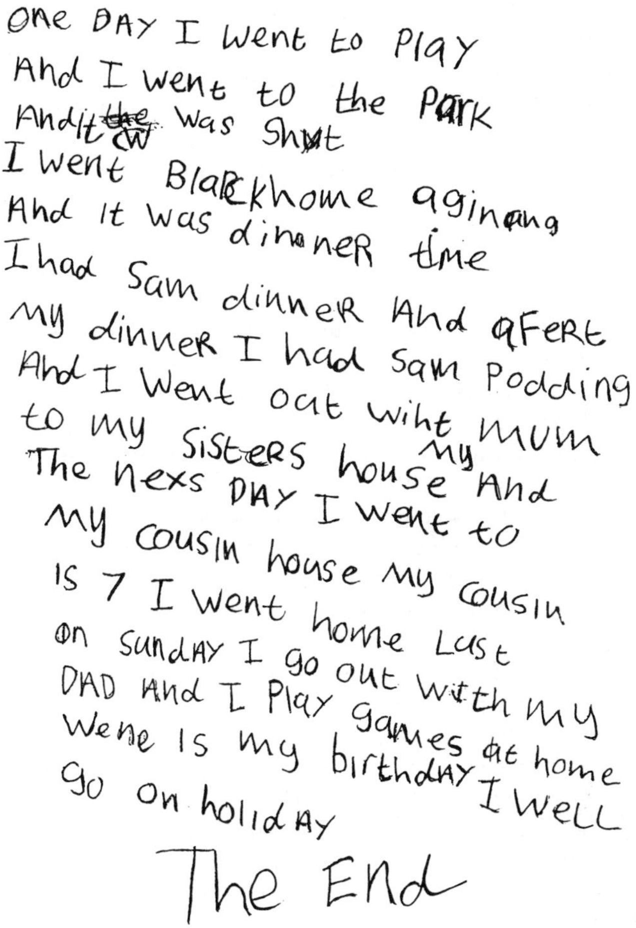

One DAY I went to Play
And I went to the Park
And it was Shut
I went Blackhome agining
And It was dinneR time
I had Sam dinneR And qFeRt
my dinneR I had Sam Podding
And I Went oat wiht mum
to my sisteRs house my And
The nexs DAY I went to
my cousin house my cousin
is 7 I went home Last
On sundAY I go out with my
DAD And I Play games at home
Wene is my birthday I well
go on holidAy
The End

Figure 3.2

was capable of drawing effectively upon a store of visual, graphophonic and morphemic information to produce close approximations to standard spelling. In addition to these developments, her demeanour as she wrote was completely different. She set about the task brimming with self-satisfied confidence, like a practised gymnast about to impress her audience with the complicated feats she was about to perform.

On the other hand, it could also be argued that the later piece had lost some of the qualities revealed in the earlier piece. With hindsight, it is possible to appreciate more fully the accomplishment reflected in the earlier piece, however reluctantly executed. Its carefully shaped structure and coherently developed single theme stand in sharp contrast to the careless arrangement of seemingly random, undeveloped themes in the later piece. There are promising traces of incipient humour and personal voice coming through in the earlier story which have all but vanished in the later one. The inclusion of make-believe beer to drink in a make-believe disco suggests a person behind the writing who is grappling, perhaps, with the frustration and envy of childhood, vicariously experiencing the pleasures and pastimes of adults, that are as yet only accessible to her through play.

This pattern of development was puzzling in view of what the research had led me to expect. If there had indeed been a loss of spark, cohesiveness and communicative power that her early writing revealed, then this was a change which could not simply be ignored. My analysis of Annette's development needed to explore how this aspect, too, of her development might be bound up with the specific features of the writing workshop that I had expected to be supportive of children's development. Might it be that the workshop's insistence on freedom of topic choice was, contrary to Graves' assumptions, having a dulling rather than an enabling effect on the content and quality of her writing? Whereas Graves' (1983) argument was that mastery of convention would follow from a strong commitment to the content of the writing, Annette's sole preoccupation seemed to be with mastering the conventions of writing, which she achieved by writing and rewriting more or less the same texts every time. I was also puzzled that what I considered to be Annette's best pieces of writing were produced in contexts where she had least ownership. Might her writing development be more effectively supported and challenged by more opportunities to write on topics prepared and stimulated by the teacher?

I decided that perhaps there was an underlying logic to these patterns of development that was not immediately obvious to me but could be discovered by probing the meaning of Annette's writing activity from her point of view. Only when I had achieved a better appreciation of what might count as progress from Annette's standpoint, taking account of her personal understanding of what she was trying to achieve with her writing, would I be in a legitimate position to assess the strengths and limitations of Annette's development as a writer and the part which the specific conditions of the writing workshop were playing in supporting, or possibly impeding, her learning.

The trouble was that Annette had never been very forthcoming about her writing in my conversations with her. Most of my information about her understandings, purposes and intentions needed to be inferred from the decisions she took, the choices she made, her spontaneous comments and requests for help, her responses to work produced, and indeed from the overall pattern emerging amongst all of these over the period of the study. The new understanding which emerged is thus still, of necessity, my own constructed version of Annette's understandings: one which seemed to me to make sense of her overall pattern of responses.

Trying to understand Annette's progress from her point of view also forced me into a narrow preoccupation with structure and convention in her writing which was decidedly alien to my own priorities and aspirations. I wanted to treat the content of her self-initiated writing as significant, and would have liked to aspire to achieve the kinds of insights of Armstrong (1980) and Steedman (1982) in their analyses of the content of children's writing. There were moments, indeed, when the content of Annette's writing did seem to be touching on significant themes, when there were flashes of insight into the person behind the writing. But the overall pattern seemed to indicate that Annette's commitment to the task of learning to write and the progress she achieved as a result were independent of a commitment to the content of her writing.

The new understanding of her learning which emerged suggested that Annette's responses were indeed intimately bound up with the specific conditions of the writing workshop, although in unexpected (and possibly unpredictable) ways. Ironically, they were directed towards coping with features of the approach (freedom of topic choice, collaboration) which I had fondly anticipated would remove obstacles to writing or enhance learning opportunities, but which it seemed, within Annette's frames of reference, themselves became transformed into sources of obstacle or threat. Nevertheless, the strategy which she devised to cope with them was not just an ingenious and effective means of making out successfully in the situation, and achieving her own purposes in learning to write. It also fortuitously created perfect conditions for Annette to repair and rebuild lost confidence, and rediscover her ability to learn through the application of her own resources.

The analysis will be presented in three parts. In the first part, I explore the connection between the overall pattern of Annette's development and the workshop's commitment to freedom of topic choice, looked at from Annette's point of view. I suggest that what enabled Annette to write with such confidence and fluency towards the end of the study was a method which she had evolved, first and foremost, as a coping strategy to help generate the content for her writing. This ensured that she always had something to write, even when she felt she had nothing to say. I trace the evolution of the method, which I call 'repertoire-writing', and show how the repetitiveness and routinization of Annette's writing which had concerned me was, in fact, an integral part of the strategy, and indeed was actually responsible for the 'remarkable progress' I had been disposed to admire.

In the second part, I examine how Annette's new commitment to work at her writing may have been bound up with the workshop's emphasis upon collaborative learning and the peer group as audience for one another's writing. I explore how this might shed further light on the development of the method and the purposes which it was serving for Annette. I also examine how this reasoning might be linked to the seeming loss of certain qualities in her writing, and what might count as progress from Annette's point of view. Then in the final part of the chapter, I return to reconsider the questions raised initially in the light of this analysis. I reassess my original assumptions about how the conditions provided by the writing workshop approach would support the learning of children who were struggling to develop their writing in the light of an assessment of the strengths and limitations of Annette's strategy. I draw out what Annette taught me about the processes of writing development, and the new questions raised by my study of her learning. I also show how the analysis serves to pinpoint new possibilities for supporting and enhancing her further development.

THE EVOLUTION OF 'REPERTOIRE – WRITING'

I shall begin by examining in more detail how Annette was able to produce with such confidence and effortless ease the second of the two pieces of writing discussed earlier. What was particularly striking about the writing was the familiarity of what she wrote, even though she had never put the words together in precisely this way before. I recognized words, phrases, structures from previous pieces of writing, some of them used many times before. It seemed that what Annette was doing was constructing a 'new' piece of writing out of the elements of previous pieces of writing, and according to a well-rehearsed format and sequence which I knew she had used many times before. Her confidence seemed to come from awareness that even a limited repertoire of words, phrases and structures can be used to generate endless variations of text, and from the conviction, confirmed by experience, that she knew how to piece them together successfully to produce a satisfactory piece of writing. Her fluency came from knowing the contents of her repertoire and its possibilities so well that, providing she had freedom to set her own topic, she could produce a page or two of text on demand, within minutes, without even having to pause for a second to think what to say.

I was sure that Annette had learnt to do these things during the period I had been observing her. She had built up her repertoire and learnt how to use it to generate fluent, extended text. How had this development been brought about and how was it bound up with the specific learning opportunities provided? Certainly, no-one had taught her this method of writing or showed her how she could use previous writing in this way. So it could reasonably be presumed to be the product of her own active intelligence, reflecting her own understandings of what the situation required and what she was trying to achieve. I decided to attempt a re-reading of the path of her development as a gradual evolution or invention of a method for writing, exploring its links with the learning conditions and opportunities provided.

Stock-taking

A few weeks into the study, and apparently quite out of the blue, Annette suddenly made a decision to dispense with drawing as a preliminary to writing. Up until now, her usual strategy had been to start by drawing a picture and then to produce a few lines of writing to accompany the picture. Thus, the week following my first sustained observations, this was again the pattern which I observed (see Figure 3.3).

A week later, however, Annette greeted my arrival with a proud announcement that she was no longer going to do drawing prior to writing. I checked with her teachers and found that this decision to abandon drawing was entirely Annette's own initiative. Though she was undoubtedly practised at reading messages about the social status of different kinds of activity, no-

Figure 3.3

one had put any pressure on her to view drawing as inappropriate or baby-ish behaviour. Indeed, even though her teachers might have actively encouraged her to spend more of her effort on writing rather than drawing, they would not have proposed abandoning drawing altogether because it was seen as providing a necessary support for writing in the early stages of development. Nevertheless, they went along with Annette's decision because they wanted to encourage her to take the initiative in her own learning.

At the time, there was no reason to suppose that this was more than a passing whim. It was significant because it was Annette's own initiative. Only with hindsight was it possible to see that this decision in fact shaped the whole course of her subsequent development. A symbolically small book had been painstakingly prepared in which the writing was to be done. Annette talked to me enthusiastically about what she planned to write about in her book, and then I remember being surprised and puzzled that what she wrote bore absolutely no resemblance to what we had discussed. I was surprised, too, that it seemed more dull than her previous writing. I was expecting, presumably, that the content would become more interesting once the writing was no longer subordinated to pictures.

However, understood as the first step in the evolution of the method, it could be that the limitation lay not in her writing but in my failure to appreciate what it was she was trying to do with her writing. Its content was actually irrelevant at this point. She was not writing to express ideas, to communicate meaning, to make meaning. She was writing to solve the problem which she had created for herself by deciding to dispense with drawing. If she was to be able to achieve this, then she had to come up with a way of managing to generate content without doing drawing. But how do you get the ideas for writing if you do not do a drawing first and then write about it? How do you know what words to write? How do you fill the page?

What Annette was doing as she filled page after page of her new book with writing was finding out if she could actually do what she planned (Figure 3.4). What is notable about these pieces is how they, already, were reworking a limited range of words, phrases and structures to produce rather similar, yet different, little texts. The writing which to me appeared rather dull and purposeless in fact had a highly significant but *different* purpose, namely to establish what Annette already knew how to write, and beginning to work out how to use this knowledge to generate ideas and resources for further writing. This was not just a matter of identifying individual words and spellings. Annette was also assembling the larger building blocks out of which continuous text was built: a sort of DIY kit of known phrases and structures (as well as individual words) which could be put together in a variety of ways to produce a piece of writing. She discovered to her satisfaction that she knew enough to cover several pages with writing. Periods of intense concentration were interspersed with bouts of gleeful counting.

In this stock-taking process, two frameworks also emerged which Annette was using to give some order and cohesion to her writing, realizing that extended text is not made up of sentences joined at random, but has some underlying principle providing structure for the writing:

'Events of the Day' structure	'About what I like' structure
1. Go somewhere	1. My (mum, dad, dog) is . . .
2. Do something	2. It is . . .
3. Return home	3. I like my . . .
4. Have something to eat	
5. Go to bed	

With one of these frameworks plus her repertoire, Annette had the means to achieve her goal of doing writing without drawing. What she had to do

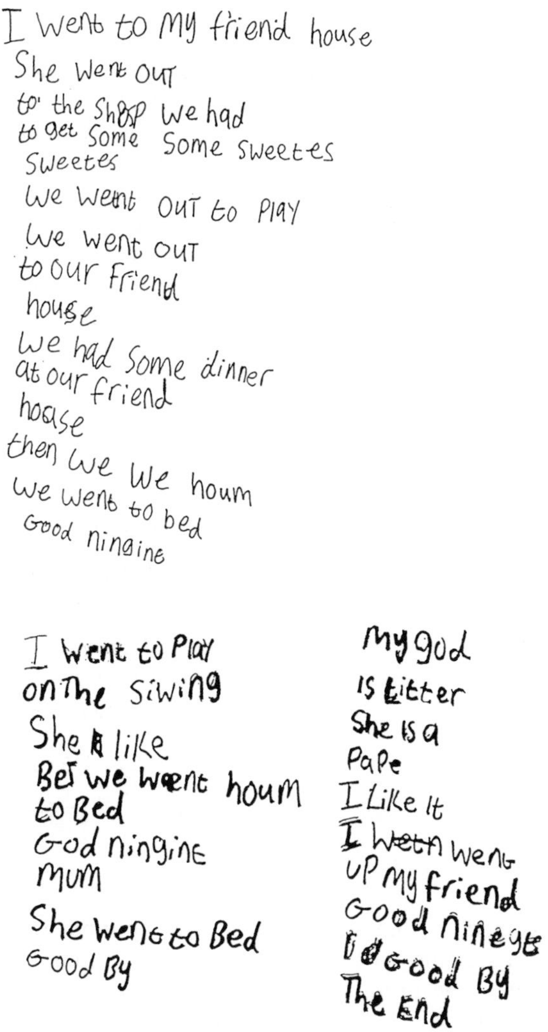

I went to my friend house
She went out
to' the shop we had
to get some some sweetes
sweetes
we went out to play
we went out
to our friend
house
we had some dinner
at our friend
house
then we we houm
we went to bed
Good ninaine

I went to play
on the siwing
She b like
Bet we went houm
to Bed
God ningine
mum

She went to Bed
Good By

my god
is Litter
She is a
Pape
I Like It
I wetn weng
up my friend
Good ninege
Good By
The End

Figure 3.4

was to follow the sequence, drawing on the contents of the repertoire, and reconstitute the elements in a variety of ways to produce 'original' pieces of writing text.

I thus located the beginnings of the method in this decision to abandon drawing as a preliminary to writing and the successful solution which Annette found to the problem which it posed. I was then puzzled, at least initially, by the seeming hiatus between this stock-taking process and the period after Christmas when repertoire-writing came into its own as Annette's principal strategy for writing. Working the thesis through, however, helped to clarify the link between the evolution of the method and the

principle of freedom of topic choice which was fundamental to the writing
workshop approach.

In the lesson immediately following the decision to abandon drawing,
Annette produced two pieces of writing: one using the events-of-the-day
framework, and one (following a conversation with her teacher) where she
used the known material in her repertoire simply as a resource for writing
about Christmas (see Figure 3.5). This was the first occasion when I was
alerted to the difference in communicative power between writing produced
on Annette's self-initiated topics and writing on themes or topics proposed

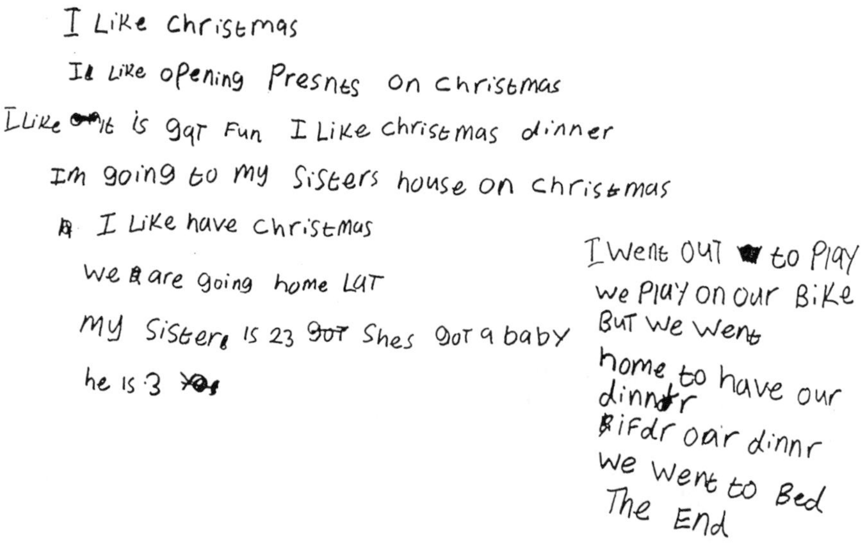

I Like Christmas

Il Like opening Presnts on christmas

ILike it is gqt Fun I Like christmas dinner

Im going to my Sisters house on christmas

A I Like have christmas

We a are going home LaT

my Sisters is 23 got Shes got a baby

he is 3 yos

I Went out to Play
we Play on our Bike
But We Went
home to have our
dinndr
if dr oair dinnr
we Went to Bed
The End

Figure 3.5

by the teacher. It seemed, at that stage, that it was the input which Annette
had received prior to starting writing which made a difference to the quality of what she wrote. The preliminary conversation with her teacher had
helped to rehearse some of the ideas, and provided Annette with some
spellings which she might require. Moreover, sensitive to Annette's desire to
identify with a more sophisticated image of herself through her writing, her
teacher (whom I shall call Linda) had also shown her how to use guidelines
under her piece of paper, to help her write straight and use up the space
right across the page.

Encouraged, perhaps, by the success of this piece, Annette continued to
base her writing on 'Christmas' over the next few writing sessions and into
the new term. Though the writing she produced was made up of many words,
phrases and structures that were familiar from previous writing, each piece
had a freshness which suggested that Annette was writing as if she had something to say (Figure 3.6).

It was when Christmas receded as a possible topic for writing, and Annette
faced the prospect of finding her own topics, as the situation required, week

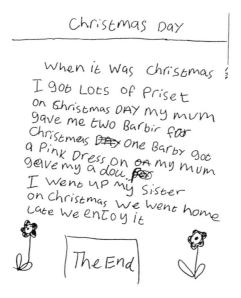

Figure 3.6

in and week out, that she appears to have turned consistently to the 'framework plus repertoire' (repertoire-writing) as a method of generating content for her writing. For the next two months, all the writing produced followed this format, creating a textual framework which relieved Annette of worry about the content of her writing, and freed her to concentrate on developing what she appeared to see as important, namely the length, fluency, accuracy in spelling and presentation of her writing.

Consolidation and extension

We can trace this process of development, using the strategy to consolidate and build the repertoire and extend the frameworks, through a number of pieces of writing carried out over a period of two months. In this text produced in early January, for example (see Figure 3.7), Annette used the basic framework to generate her writing, drawing upon the contents of the repertoire selectively, and with considerable repetition, to ensure that most of what she wrote was made up of known material. She used a total of 32 individual words, some repeated, making a total of 71 words in all. Of these, she could produce 22 in standard form without assistance, leaving herself free to concentrate on the spelling of just ten words. Of these, four were words which she had used previously but was still working on. By re-using them in this new context, she was bringing her spelling of them to a closer approximation to standard spelling. Her unaided efforts (on rough paper) produced 'fandr' for 'friend', 'dinr' for 'dinner', 'nitr' for 'night' and 'pick' for 'park'. She also practised using the body of known material which she was begin-

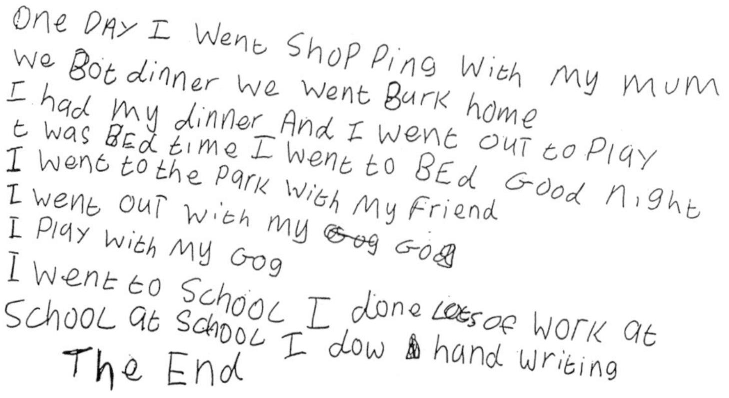

One DAY I Went Shopping With my mum
We Bot dinner we went Bark home
I had my dinner And I went out to Play
t was BEd time I went to BEd Good night
I went to the Park With My Friend
I went out with my dog dog
I Play with my Gog
I went to School
School at School I done Lots of Work at
School at School I dow a hand writing
The End

Figure 3.7

ning to accumulate, to attempt some unfamiliar words which, to my knowledge, had not so far appeared in her writing ('shoppen' for 'shopping', 'witaing' for 'writing', 'winv' for 'with', 'dow' for 'done', 'bot' for 'bought' and 'bark' for 'back').

Thus, through this piece, Annette was able not just to consolidate and develop her knowledge of particular words but also to begin to generate hypotheses about sound-symbol relationships which would facilitate the spelling of words she was using for the first time. Within the safety of the overall framework, she also permitted herself to experiment ever so slightly with new words and formulations which varied and extended structures which she had used previously. In the first sentence, for example, she tried out the use of 'one day' as a possible opening phrase (inappropriately, as it happens, in this piece). The basic narrative element 'I went to . . .' is reformulated here as 'I went shopping', adding (for the first time) with my mum, and later (with the same verb) 'with my friend' and 'with my dog'. 'Back' also appears for the first time in the phrase 'we went back home'. These new elements were all to become regular features of subsequent writing.

Perhaps inspired by the success of this practice and limited experimentation, Annette then, in the final two lines, departed entirely from previous content to include (still in the routine framework) reference to life in school. This was the first, and indeed the only occasion when Annette chose to make any reference to school learning in her writing. Thus, repertoire-writing did not entirely limit or circumscribe her writing. It could be argued, on the contrary, that it was the safety, support and confidence generated by the framework that created the possibility to take risks, without fear of failure. That Annette herself was indeed feeling a sense of satisfaction in her achievement was confirmed a week later, when she turned to me spontaneously and said, 'I'm getting the hang of it now.'

Three weeks later, the same overall framework was perceptible, but many new elements were introduced (see Figure 3.8). In the opening sequence of

One DAY I went UP My
frinds house her name is Joann
we PlaY Gams And I Like PlaYing
games with my frind it was
dinner time I went home to
have My dinner we PlaYd out
agen I went to The SoPs with
my MuM BouTe
My DAD tolk me OuT
I Like My DAD went Back home
It was bed time

The End

Goodd BYe

Figure 3.8

the events-of-the-day narrative, the basic format has been noticeably expanded:

Basic structure	New structure
1. Go somewhere	1. Go somewhere
2. Do something	2. Say something about it
3. Return home	3. Do something
	4. Say something about it
	5. Time for a meal

This elaboration of the basic narrative framework may have been influenced by Annette's experience in producing two pieces of curriculum-related descriptive writing (see Figure 3.9 and Figure 3.10). This work also seems

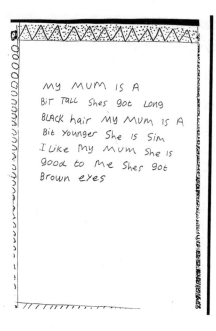

MY MUM IS A
BIT TALL Shes got Long
BLACK hair MY MUM IS A
Bit Younger She is Sim
I Like MY MUM She is
good to Me Shes got
Brown eyes

Figure 3.9

MY name is Rose 1 am 42 I
got two Chilaren I work in The
Pet Shop IV got A pet At home
it is a dog dog dog come And
See come And See A nother
dog

Figure 3.10

to have suggested to Annette the possibility of incorporating elements of her alternative framework 'about what I like' into the basic narrative framework. However, elaborating the basic structures of her writing did not appear to be a conscious priority for Annette at this stage, perhaps more an unconscious influence arising from her other writing experience. Spelling was still her main preoccupation and concern, and the sole area where she actively sought help and support for her writing.

New applications

The evolution of the method and its possibilities for generating writing appeared to enter a new phase with Annette's shift to writing in the third person. This shift may also have been suggested by curriculum-related work, but was clearly a deliberate decision which Annette continued to pursue and explore for several weeks (see Figure 3.11). With this shift, she suddenly discovered that the routines of the repertoire could be used to make texts that were not just about Annette herself and the real everyday events of her life. The writing begins with an impressive, story-like opening, quite unlike anything she had written so far. After the three opening moves, however, real-

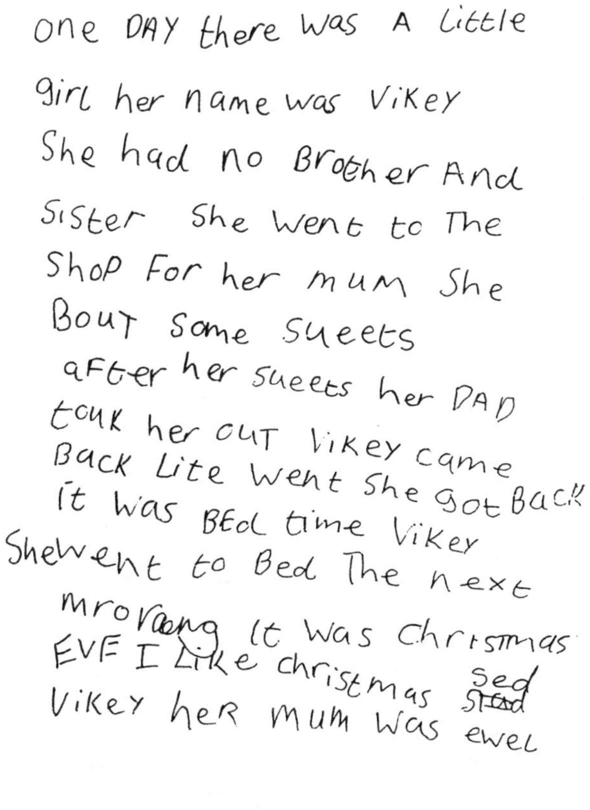

One DAY there was A Little
girl her name was ViKey
She had no Brother And
Sister She Went to The
Shop For her mum She
Bout Some Sueets
after her sueets her DAD
touk her ouT likey came
Back Lite Went She got Back
It Was BEd time Viker
Shewent to Bed The next
mrovong It Was Christmas
EVE I Like christmas Sed
Vikey heR mum was ewel

Figure 3.11

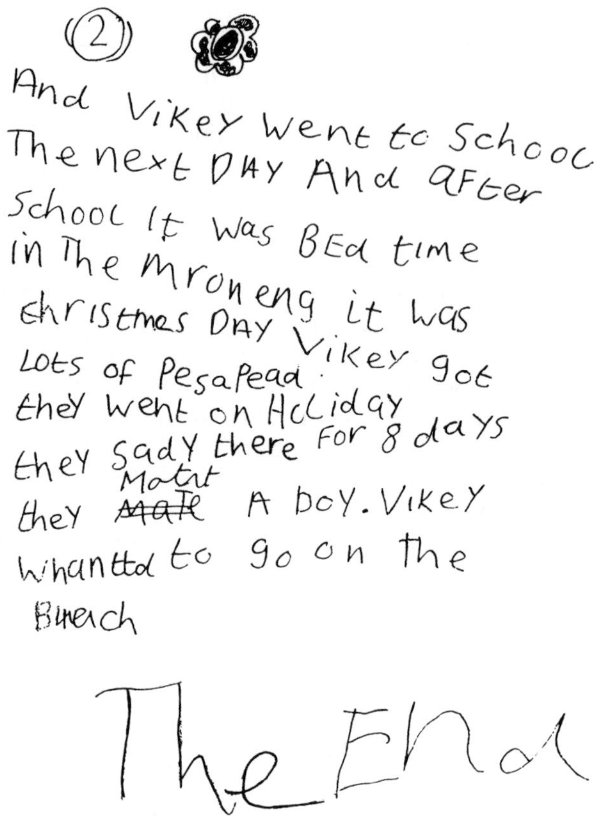

(2)

And Vikey Went to Schoo
The next DAY And after
School It Was BEd time
in The mroneng it was
christmes DAY Vikey got
Lots of Pesapead.
they went on HoLiday
they sadY there For 8 days
they Matit
they Matit A boY. VikeY
Whanttd to go on the
Bireach

The End

Figure 3.11 (cont)

izing perhaps that she was unable to continue in the genre, the text reverts
to the routines of the repertoire. It seems as if Annette suddenly discovered
that she could re-use all her previous writing about herself, to generate content for 'made-up' writing. The effect was liberating. Instantly, she produced
two pages of writing, where previously she had been satisfied with one. The
events-of-the day had to be extended to include 'the next morning' and 'the
next day', which appeared in her writing for the first time.

Thus, the discovery of third-person writing opened up a whole new dimension to Annette's writing-learning strategy. Writing in the third person created new scope for using, consolidating and further extending the repertoire,
while opening up new opportunities that were not available in its first person application. In this first attempt at a third-person story, Annette found
herself having to explore adjustments that needed to be made to the routines of the repertoire at the level of pronouns; she also experimented with
the use of speech for the first time ('I like Christmas, said Vikey'). Then, in
the way that success previously bred the confidence to take risks, she was
further inspired, it seems, to experiment in the last part of the story

with four original sentences which bore no direct relationship to previous work.

Her experiment with third-person writing continued for the next few weeks, and I was surprised therefore that she suddenly reverted to first person writing for the penultimate piece of the study discussed earlier (see Figure 3.12, also Figure 3.2). Perhaps she had exhausted for the time being the possibilities of writing in the third person, aware that she did not really know, beyond her framework, how to structure an extended piece of narrative. Through the practice provided by this experience, however, she had so firmly consolidated the repertoire and her own facility in using it, that the text virtually wrote itself from her available resources.

We have now traced the processes by which Annette came to acquire the confidence, knowledge and skills which allowed her to write on this occa-

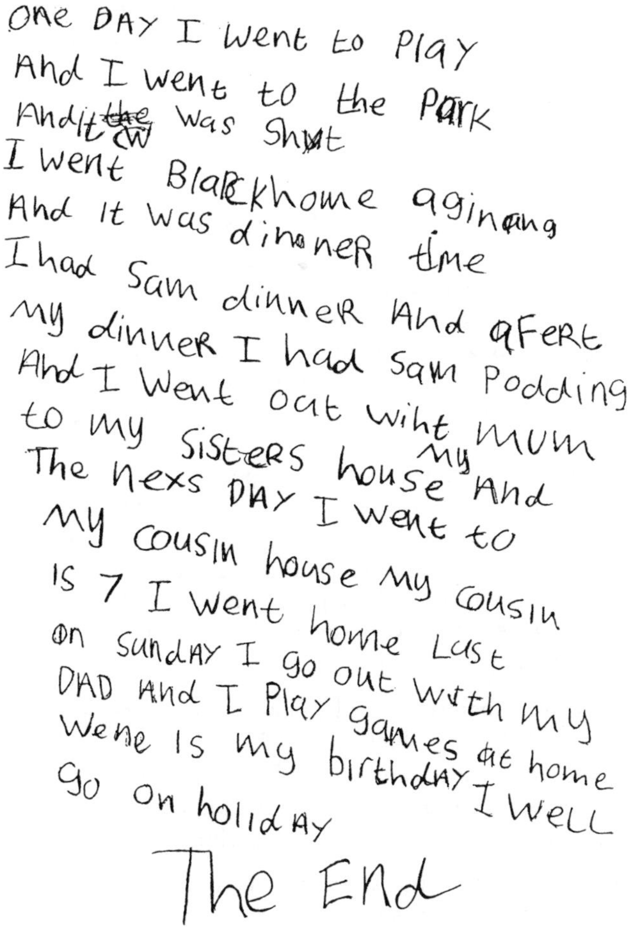

One DAY I went to Play
And I went to the Park
And it was shut
I went Blackhome aginang
And it was dinner time
I had Sam dinner And afert
my dinner I had Sam Podding
And I went out wiht my mum
to my Sisters house And
The nexs DAY I went to
my cousin house my cousin
is 7 I went home Last
On Sunday I go out with my
DAD And I Play games at home
Wene is my birthday I well
go on holiday

The End

Figure 3.12

sion with such ease and fluency. The piece demonstrates the control which Annette was by now able to exercise over her own writing, and the knowledge base now available to her as a resource for future learning. It confirms the success which Annette has had in her efforts to bring her spelling of some familiar, often used words to standard form. For example, if we compare this piece to one carried out two months earlier (Figure 3.7), we find that:

- 'pick' has become 'park'
- 'dinr' has become 'dinner'
- 'winv' has become 'with' (also 'wiht').

We can see the wisdom of creating opportunities for constant repetition of the same words in order to consolidate her knowledge of standard spellings, since some of the words which she is still working on in this piece are ones which she has already used many times before and written in standard form, e.g.:

- 'nexs' for 'next'
- 'sam' for 'some'
- 'afert' for 'after'

However, there was also evidence that Annette was not simply relying on learning to spell by committing to memory previously seen or provided words. She was using her existing knowledge to begin to generate an understanding of sound–symbol relationships which she could use to make a reasonable attempt at unknown or unfamiliar words. For example, the use of 'r' to represent sounds in 'birthday' ('brthday') and 'holiday' ('holrday') show Annette actively problem-solving and coming up with her own generalizations to aid her in her spelling.

Thus Annette's new confidence came, perhaps, at the most fundamental level, from the rediscovery of her own ability to learn through the exercise of her existing resources. As a result of her own initiative in deciding to rework continually the same themes and routines, she now had a growing body of knowledge which could support her in any task of writing as well as helping her generate new understandings of how the writing system worked. This included:

- a body of known material (words, phrases, structures and frameworks for building extended text) which she could use directly in her writing;
- an emerging set of understandings and generalizations about how the written code operates derived from this body of known material which allowed her to generate new hypotheses and experiment with unfamiliar material.

It struck me, in fact, that the strategy which Annette had devised for herself, and which had proved so effective in bringing about certain sorts of learning was not so different from the task of 'writing news' which children are often asked to do on a regular basis in the early years of writing development. The key difference, though, in Annette's case, was that the strategy was her own idea, her own way of coping and responding to the needs of the situation. If it had been proposed by one of her teachers, it almost certainly would not have been helpful at all because the underlying rationale would have come from their understandings and purposes, not hers. Annette would have been working to the teacher's agenda (and submitting to the teacher's expectations and control) rather than her own.

Intimately bound up, then, with the principle of freedom of topic choice, the appeal of repertoire-writing for Annette was no doubt that it removed the terror of being confronted with a blank page and, within limits, guaranteed successful writing every time. It was an ingenious strategy for a 'person without turf', ensuring that she always had something to write, even when she felt she had nothing to say. Graves (1983) does indeed acknowledge the problems that freedom of topic choice may create for children who do not feel they have anything to write about:

> Children who feel as though they know nothing or have had no significant experiences in their lives, are up against it when given personal choice with topics in writing. Many children have had it knocked into them by parents, other children and a succession of teachers that there is little of significance to their lives. Topical choice for these children can be devastating.
>
> (Graves, 1983, p. 27).

Topic choice was never 'devastating' for Annette because she worked out a way round it. Repertoire-writing was a substitute: a way of not having to worry about having a topic for writing. Indeed, it was so successful that, remarkably in my experience, there was only one occasion throughout the whole period of the study when Annette appealed for help because she was at a loss for something to write about or what to say next.

However, repertoire-writing was more than just a means of getting by, in the sense of fulfilling the day-to-day expectations on each child to produce some writing. Quite apart from the repeated experience of success which it provided, which was itself not insignificant, the opportunity for constant reworking of the same material which it provided also proved to be a powerful strategy for growth. It allowed her to hold constant what she knew for long enough to consolidate and gradually extend her existing knowledge and skills and to begin to generate once more her own hypotheses about how the writing system worked. Whether by coincidence, judgement, or a fortuitous combination of circumstances, repertoire-writing provided the means for Annette gradually to regain a sense of control over what she knew, and to rediscover how to use what she knew to foster her own learning.

My conclusion so far is that the strategy which was responsible for Annette's progress was bound up with the conditions of the workshop approach in two ways. It was a *response* to the expectation that children would choose their own topics for writing; and it was *made possible* by the principle that children should control their own writing . However, this is clearly only part of the story. Annette could perfectly well have continued to generate her topics for writing via drawing, as no-one was putting any pressure on her to dispense with drawing as a preliminary to writing. What was it, then, that prompted this decision at this particular time, and how did the thinking behind it help to shape the subsequent course of Annette's writing development?

A SELF-PROTECTIVE STRATEGY?

I had been aware that Annette's relationships with other children in her own class were difficult. She had just one friend, Angie, who was in a parallel class and who was allowed to come and join her for writing workshop sessions as their teachers felt this was beneficial. On one occasion Annette complained to me that other children made fun of her work and, from what she said, it seemed that she was not referring to an isolated event. However, it did not occur to me to make a connection between problems in Annette's social relationships and the pattern of her writing development until I noticed that the decision to abandon drawing coincided with a moment of known crisis in her relationships with other children.

Just before she made the decision, Annette had had a row with Angie and told me that they were no longer speaking to one another. Whilst this is a slim basis of evidence upon which to build a theory, it nevertheless provided an interesting line of enquiry to pursue. I suddenly realized how exposed it must feel to be a child with limited writing competence in the context of the writing workshop, and how much more vulnerable still would be a child who was socially isolated, and therefore unsure who could be counted upon to give her work a sympathetic hearing. Although, in any classroom, children have sight of one another's work and make judgements about one another's ability, in the writing workshop this exposure is part of the formal rather than the hidden curriculum. Children are expected to share their writing with one another, to ask questions, make judgements about one another's work, to help one another with their writing and to provide an audience for one another. This is intended to create an ethos of shared endeavour and mutual respect '. . . a group force that lifts each child, no matter what his ability' (Graves, 1983, p. 42).

I had assumed, on the basis of previous research, reading and experience, that a collaborative ethos would be helpful and supportive to children experiencing difficulties, ensuring that they were not left to struggle on alone. Yet I began to see that from Annette's point of view it could be more of a threat than an opportunity. Having, temporarily at least, lost the protection of Angie, Annette was suddenly without a single advocate in a situation of high exposure. It may have been this which not only precipitated her into taking an initiative with her writing, but played a key role in determining the form of that initiative.

Moreover, I discovered a second occasion, too, when a significant point of growth in her writing coincided with a moment of crisis in her relationships with other children. Just before the shift to third-person writing, I observed a group of girls making thinly disguised fun of Annette's writing while pretending to respond positively to it. I began to explore the possibility that Annette's decision to abandon drawing and the focus of her subsequent concerns in learning to write might have been prompted, at least in part, by a desire to protect herself against teasing and unkind taunts by raising her status in the eyes of peers, at a time when she felt particularly isolated and vulnerable.

The precise form which her initiative took, in the decision to abandon drawing, was perfectly adapted to such a motivation. Its immediate practical effect was to transform the visible features of Annette's writing, making it less likely to attract unwanted attention and possible ridicule. The particular characteristics and strengths of repertoire-writing also fit admirably with such a rationale. As a coping and learning strategy, it was perfectly adapted to enabling Annette to develop, as quickly as possible, the ability to produce a page of text with fluency and accuracy (which, it seems, was her model of 'good writing'). This interpretation would thus be consistent with Annette's single-minded concern with convention and seeming lack of interest in the content or quality of her writing throughout the period of the study. Certainly, content and meaning did not figure at all in her conscious concerns during this period, as reflected in her comments, questions, requests for help and changes which she made to her own writing. She seemed to be concerned simply with quantity, presentation and accuracy of spelling. The problems which she struggled to solve and strategies which she experimented with were bound up with mastery of convention, rather than a struggle to make meaning.

Repertoire-writing ensured that she was not held up from achieving her own purposes because she could not think of ideas to write or because she did not yet know how to structure extended writing. The means by which it achieved this, however, led to the seeming loss of spark, shape and communicative power in her self-initiated writing. We can now, perhaps, better appreciate the mysterious reappearance of these qualities where (according to Graves) they ought to be least in evidence, namely in writing tasks or topics set or proposed not by Annette but by her teacher (see Figure 3.13).

It seemed that these qualities reappeared in Annette's texts when she had

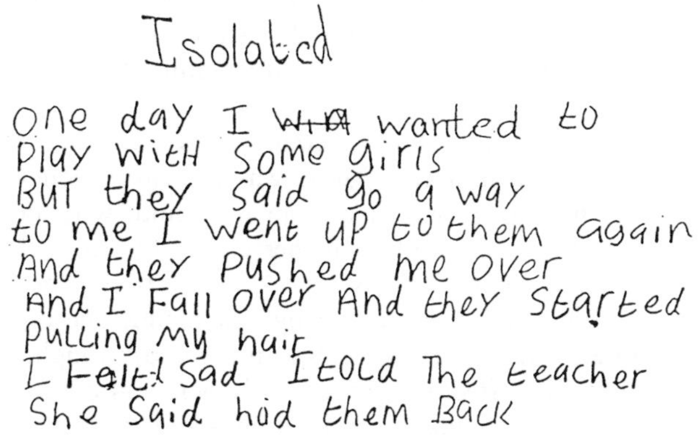

Isolated

One day I ~~wra~~ wanted to
Play WitH Some girls
But they said go a way
to me I went uP to them again
And they Pushed me over
And I Fall over And they Started
Pulling My hair
I Felt sad I told The teacher
She said had them Back

Figure 3.13

a clear sense of topic to give shape to her writing, which was precisely what repertoire-writing did not provide. For example, a piece written in early January (Figure 3.13) uses many words from Annette's repertoire, but succeeds in using them to tell a fully formed story in which the pain of isolation (a daily reality for Annette, as has been explained) comes across powerfully. It provides a sharp contrast with Annette's self-initated writing, where sentences tend to be juxtaposed in what Applebee (1978) calls 'heaps' or 'sequences', i.e. relatively disconnected collections of sentences with little cohesive structure. Here, on the contrary, there is an opening sequence to set the scene, a gradual build-up of tension to a climax, the denouement followed by a final resolution. Sentences are all logically interconnected with effective use of cohesive ties. The whole story centres on just one brief incident, whereas frequently in Annette's repertoire-writing one flat sentence is intended to represent hours and hours of time.

When Annette made the decision, for her own reasons, to abandon drawing as a preliminary to writing, she also unwittingly rid herself of an essential support which gave a necessary shape, structure and coherence to her writing and which she was not yet ready to provide for herself unaided. Initially, this was not so obvious, because the arrival of Christmas brought an immediate supply of themes which continued to support Annette in the same way. However, as repertoire-writing became her main strategy, the difference in quality and coherence between her self-initiated writing and teacher-led writing became increasingly noticeable.

This contrast is even more convincingly illustrated in her final piece of writing, produced just one week after the triumphant demonstration of competence discussed earlier, in response to an invitation to write a letter for a teacher who was leaving (see Figure 3.14). Writing this letter was far more challenging than anything she had previously attempted. It involved a struggle from which she almost withdrew defeated. In total contrast to the previous week when she had been so confident and competent, this week she appeared to be deflated, irritable, disinclined to work. The idea of attempting a letter was perhaps so terrifying that initially she declared that she was not going to write one. She spent a good portion of the lesson designing an elaborate border for her sheet of paper, and claiming that she needed to start it all over again.

When she finally took the plunge, seized her pen and began to write, the process was painful and hesitant. Gone was the easy fluency of the previous week. Words had to be wrestled from her mind, with much attendant stress and anxiety that she would find herself unable to complete the task after all. For the first time since my initial observations, she was explicitly asking for help with what to write, though each time she rejected my suggestions and came up with her own ideas. In the end, though, she succeeded in producing a moving, effective and intensely personal communication to a teacher who had given her much sensitive help and encouragement.

It was this piece of writing which, by my criteria, seemed best to bear witness to the progress which Annette had made in her writing since my ear-

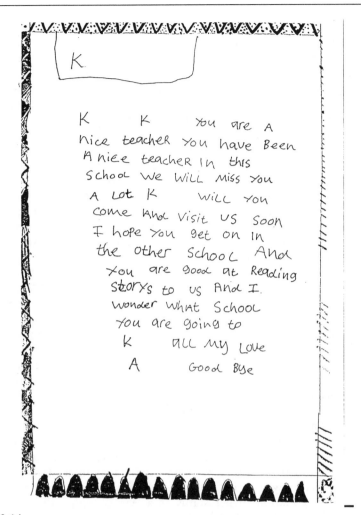

Figure 3.14

liest encounters with her. It was hard to imagine that the girl who had laboured to produce the 'disco' piece could have even attempted, let alone successfully accomplished, a letter of this nature. Yet the struggle and frustration involved for Annette was as great, if not greater – certainly more prolonged – than on that first occasion. We can thus appreciate the contribution that repertoire-writing was making to her writing development, and so avoid simplistic comparisons between Annette's self-initiated and teacher-initiated writing. There was little doubt that she could not have sustained her commitment to learning to write, if all her writing experiences had presented this level of frustration. Indeed, without the confidence and resources produced through her repertoire-writing strategy, she would undoubtedly not have been able to attempt this tribute to her teacher.

To contrast the quality of pieces produced through repertoire-writing with teacher-initiated writing, according to some abstract criteria of 'quality', was to misunderstand both the difference and the interdependence between the two sorts of writing. What Annette was doing when she was repertoire-writing was *practising* writing. She was generating the knowledge, skills and confidence to be able to attempt, with reasonable competence and success, the 'real' writing requirements of school. Putting these resources to work on teacher-proposed curriculum topics provided enough of a challenge to stimulate development, and a sense of increasing ability to rise to meet the challenge, which in turn reinforced her willingness to engage in further practice.

Indeed, I now realize that Annette indicated this to me herself, in so many words, in an exchange that took place a couple of weeks after Annette had made her shift to third-person writing. For the first time in four months, she had spent time drawing a picture before starting to write. Annette showed me her picture of the two girls, and I said without thinking, 'Are you going to write a story about them?' Annette said, 'No, just writing'.

The words took me aback in their unexpectedly literal response to my carelessly worded question. What I really meant to say was, 'What are you going to write about?', using the concept of 'story' loosely to refer to any kind of composition of the child's creation. Annette, however, was clearly making much finer discriminations. She knew that what she would write was not really a 'story', but her tone appeared to be asserting that this did not actually matter. Far from apologizing for 'just writing', she regarded it as an altogether legitimate activity. It was only when she was 'just writing' that she could display the confidence, fluency and accuracy to which she aspired, and which were necessary to reinforce her sense of her own competence in her own eyes and, even more importantly, perhaps, in the eyes of others. She knew that she had achieved the ability to do this through her own endeavours, and for the time being that was quite achievement enough.

My conclusion, then, is that we might legitimately understand the overall course of Annette's writing development during the period of the study as a process of renegotiation of her status as a learner within the class group. Her self-devised strategy played a key role in this process. Both task and strategy were intimately bound up with the conditions of the writing workshop, albeit in unexpected and somewhat ambiguous ways. Freedom of topic choice provided both the opportunity and the occasion for the development of the strategy, while social pressures of collaborative learning both prompted and shaped the evolution of the strategy. Though Annette's relationships remained problematic up to the point where she left, at the end of the Spring term, she was certainly successful in achieving progress in writing in her own terms. Whatever reservations I might have about the means by which she achieved this, and the implications for further development, I have no doubt that the process served the most important goal of all, from a teacher's point of view: namely to allow Annette to regain control of what she knew and how to use what she knew independently to foster further learning.

THE TEACHER'S PERSPECTIVE

Having attempted to understand the meaning of Annette's writing activity from her point of view, I shall now return to my own teacher perspective and consider what has been learnt from the experience in terms of my own understandings and questions.

During the course of the analysis, my original doubts about Annette's progress, reflected in two different perceptions of the changes that had occurred over the period of the study, have been resolved, as the perceptions themselves have been challenged and the inter-relationship between them better understood from Annette's point of view. The new confidence and fluency that I originally saw as signs of progress were found to be dependent upon the use of the method, and so were demonstrated only in those practice situations where the method could be directly applied. The dull repetitiveness of her writing that concerned me was found to be the means by which Annette achieved her confidence and fluency, and indeed the means by which she achieved the increased mastery of convention that had so impressed me. The seeming loss of positive qualities, too, simply reflected the loss of in-built structural support for Annette's writing provided by a drawing or theme, not loss of qualities reflecting Annette's (implicit or explicit) compositional knowledge, or commitment to her writing.

However, whilst the analysis has helped to resolve those particular doubts, it has helped to make concrete in a different way my uneasy sense that there was something about the way that Annette had chosen to exercise control that was not altogether serving the best interests of her writing development. The new tension which has emerged between the functions of repertoire-writing as a *coping strategy* and as a *learning strategy* is particularly helpful, because it allows me to distinguish between, on the one hand, appreciation and acknowledgement of the competence, ingenuity and astute assessment of personal need revealed in Annette's self-devised strategy, while on the other hand recognizing its limitations with regard to her learning.

Taking my lead from Holt's (1969) uncomfortably telling analysis of the ways children find to cope with the demands of school learning, my analysis of Annette's strategy recognizes that children may use their ingenuity in ways which are not only at odds with their teacher's aspirations and purposes, but also impede their own learning. In my account, though, repertoire-writing is a more ambiguous strategy. It enables Annette to cope and, through coping, to learn. It also enables Annette to cope and, through coping, to side-step the need to develop her resources in certain areas. Part of its function as a coping strategy was to compensate for the knowledge, skills and resources which Annette did not have (or thought she did not have) and still be successful in her own terms. By enabling Annette to manage without, rather than develop, these resources, yet still achieve her own purposes and meet the expectations of the situation, the strategy was also actively impeding her learning in some areas. More worrying, perhaps, its very success in enabling Annette to manage without these resources (and indeed to make remarkable progress) tended to obscure their absence and therefore fail to alert teachers to what further steps they might want to take to support their development.

For example, by helping Annette, a 'person without turf', to generate content for writing, it allowed Annette to overcome the fear that she had nothing to write about, but *obscured* her need to learn to value and use her own knowledge and experience as a resource for writing. By providing a simple narrative framework, it allowed Annette to produce extended texts that had the appearance of a kind of development and structure, but *obscured* Annette's need to learn what is involved in producing more elaborated writing. And by allowing her to produce 'successful' texts, without concern for content, it tended to reinforce her limited, utilitarian view about what writing is and what it is for, and *denied* her the opportunity to experience the real basis for decision-making in the construction of a text.

Thus although Annette's strategy was closely bound up with features of the writing workshop, some of the ways in which it contributed to her progress seemed to be significantly at odds with Graves' thesis about how the conditions of the writing workshop would support children's writing development. According to this, freedom of topic choice would help to generate a strong commitment on the part of the child to what she had to say. This commitment to the topic would then both generate the problems to be solved (with the teacher's help and instruction) and sustain the child as she worked at solving the problems involved in realizing her ideas and intentions in writing. The process of solving the problems would provide the cutting edge for learning and the focus for teaching. Learning the conventions of writing was integral to and dependent upon this process.

According to my interpretation, however, Annette's purposes for writing and her commitment to learning were not connected to expressive or communicative intentions of her own. She showed little sign of the inner urge to write claimed by Calkins (1986, p. 3):

> Human beings have a deep need to represent their experiences through writing . . . By articulating experience, we reclaim it for ourselves. Writing allows us to turn the chaos into something beautiful, to frame selected moments in our lives, to uncover and celebrate the organising patterns of our experience.

As far as it was possible to tell, her understanding of the task of learning to write seemed to be limited to the mastery of convention, and her sense of the purposes of learning to write limited to a purely utilitarian focus upon what was required of her in school. She generated a commitment to learning to write and found a means of developing her mastery of convention in spite of, or perhaps even (paradoxically) *because of*, paying no attention to the content of her writing. My story of her learning has explored how this was possible, the influences which may have led her to exercise control in this way, and the advantages as well as the disadvantages of her learning strategy.

There were still doubts in my mind as to whether these features of her writing *were* actually problematic or whether I had a vested interest in *finding* something problematic in order to explore possibilities for development.

In my work as a teacher, rather than as a researcher, I would have been delighted to celebrate the success of the child, and would have not wanted to diminish this by pointing out what had yet to be accomplished. This could be taken care of later, once the child was back on a positive path to independent learning.

Annette's choice to limit her writing to a narrow range of topics could simply be seen as a legitimate instance of what Graves (1983, p. 241) calls 'centering': 'Writers of all kinds can only focus on so much at a time. General, even specific centering, such as focusing on the same topic or using the same words, can become holding patterns for other kinds of growth.' Her preoccupation with convention could be seen as an inevitable feature of the early stages of writing development, since children cannot give their attention to the content of writing while so much of their efforts are bound up with the mechanics of writing:

> Most beginners . . . cite spelling as the center issue. . . This is because so much of their problem solving is simply at the spelling level. Until the word is spelled completely, neither the child, nor friends or teachers will be able to understand the message. Next the child moves on to aesthetics and form – 'What is the best way to put it down and be neat?' – and moves on to a new type of convention. . . When the child has put the conventions as well as the motor-aesthetic issues well behind him, more attention should be given to the topic and information.
>
> (Graves, 1983, pp. 235–6)

However, I resisted the temptation to silence my concerns in this way, even though the analysis seemed to be moving perilously close to the re-introduction of a deficit interpretation of Annette's learning, because it seemed to me that to do so would not be in Annette's best interests. She needed to develop, not manage without the resources which repertoire-writing was designed to compensate for, and it seemed unlikely that she would take this initiative herself, since she had removed the incentive to do so by devising repertoire-writing.

Teachers would not necessarily see the need for such an initiative if we were to assume on the basis of her progress (and Graves' reassurances) that all was well. In that case, we would not only overlook opportunities to intervene effectively to support and enhance Annette's learning, but also fail to be alerted to ways in which limitations in the learning conditions provided may have helped to create the need to compensate for limited resources in the first place.

IMPLICATIONS FOR PRACTICE

It seemed to me that it would be in Annette's interests to take seriously the limitations as well as the strengths of her learning strategy. We would need to look carefully at the limitations in her current resources which shaped the design of the strategy, consider what might be learnt from these about the adequacy of conditions currently provided and what adjustment or developments might need to be introduced to support Annette's learning in the areas identified. It may indeed be that, in the process, we come to revise our perception of those limitations but in ways that open up rather than close off new learning opportunities for Annette and for ourselves.

> All literary texts are woven out of other literary texts, not in the conventional sense that they bear the traces of 'influence' but in the more radical sense that every word, phrase or segment is a reworking of other writings which precede or surround the individual work. There is no such thing as the 'first' literary work: all literature is intertextual.
>
> (Eagleton, 1983, p. 138)

I came to realize, for example, that what Annette was doing in constructing new texts from the words, phrases and structures of previously written and encountered texts was, in some respects, similar to what *all* writers do. Although I reacted with some ambivalence to Annette's routines, feeling with discomfort that she was misunderstanding the whole point of writing, she had in fact begun to work out for herself a fundamental principle of writing now widely acknowledged in the literature, although it had not previously occurred to me, in so many words, (nor, as far as I am aware, is any mention made in Graves' and Calkins' work). As Rosen points out below, all writers work from a repertoire. For all of us, textual possibilities are already pre-inscribed on the page. What varies, for each of us, is what is in the repertoire and the uses to which we put it to realize our intentions:

> What is pre-inscribed on the page is different for each one of us. Never to have encountered the classic folk tale or blank verse is to have these forms erased from the page. There is gain and loss. On the one hand the writer is released from the tyranny of the model and on the other is more limited in choice and support. As the pen moves and pauses, the writer is making choice after choice, powerfully affected by the already inscribed invisible texts.
>
> (Rosen, 1992, p. 128)

Following this view, then, the task would be not so much to prise Annette gradually away from reliance on the strategy but rather to help her enhance the *content* of the repertoire and learn how to use it more effectively in the service of meaning-making rather than, as currently, as a *substitute* for meaning-making. One limitation of Annette's current concept of repertoire was that she appeared to assume that it should only contain resources drawn from her own previous writing, and not from other texts encountered, books she had read or stories read aloud. Perhaps previous experience of school where it was right to 'do your own work' and wrong to 'copy from books' had misled her into thinking that she could not draw legitimately on other people's writing, upon books read and stories listened to, as resources for her own writing.

She needed to have the process of 'reading in the role of the writer' (Smith, 1983) introduced to her, so that she could be alert to new resources arising from her reading encounters which might be added to her repertoire and subsequently used in her writing. The organization of the writing workshop may in fact unwittingly inhibit children from making this link between reading and writing. Because time for writing is scheduled separately from reading and other curriculum activities, an artificial separation is created which could inhibit children from realizing not just that they can, but that they should, use ideas drawn from reading in their writing. It is notable that, in their more recent writings, Graves (1989) and Calkins (1991) have taken up this issue themselves and given more attention to the range of experiences which may need to be provided to help children grasp the interdependent relationship between reading and writing.

It is questionable, though, whether children can derive the knowledge that they need about how different kinds of texts are put together from reading in this way. As well as being limited by the range of resources in her repertoire, Annette's writing was also limited by only having one framework around which to structure her texts. We saw her making her first move to experiment with third-person story genre, beginning convincingly with three opening sentences firmly located in the genre, and then discovering that she did not know how to continue. She was happy to settle for 'just writing', for the time being, but how would she be able to acquire the knowledge about how to structure a story and elaborate her meanings that she currently lacked?

The questions raised by Annette's case thus take us to the heart of the current controversies amongst educationalists in the field about the teaching of 'genre' (e.g. Kress, 1982; Christie, 1990; Littlefair, 1993; Rosen, 1992). On the one hand, it is argued that some children (and particularly those with limited reading skills) will be disadvantaged if we leave them to pick this up for themselves through their encounters with reading. On the other hand, it is claimed that explicit teaching of genres will lead to writing which is unadventurous, stereotyped, lacking in creativity. It is interesting to note that, in terms of absolute, external criteria, much of Annette's writing displayed these qualities, in spite of learning to write in a situation where no specific presentation of 'models' for writing was provided.

Certainly, Annette's classroom did provide specific opportunities for children to participate in group story-writing led by a teacher and explicitly designed to encourage children to talk about the choices which a writer makes in composition. This may indeed have been, at least in part, what prompted Annette to attempt to write her own third-person story. Nevertheless, the story which the group produced was very long, and the processes of its production may have been too complex at this stage of Annette's development for her to draw out key ideas which she could apply in her own writing.

It is difficult to know whether, for Annette, the problem was one of knowing how to structure a piece of writing or simply not trying to write about anything in particular. When writing about a drawing or theme, and when she had a clear sense what there was to say about the topic, the structure seemed to follow from the development of the ideas. It is possible that encouraging Annette to write on specific topics or themes, and using her experience of texts read or heard read aloud as a guide, would be sufficient support for her writing at this stage. Certainly, it is beyond the scope of this chapter, and indeed this study, to pursue the 'genre' debate here. It is noted simply as an illustration of the kinds of complex curriculum questions, for which there are no simple solutions, which might need to be pursued as a result of studying one child's learning.

It brings us back, however, to perhaps the fundamental problem of persuading a 'person without turf' that she has something worthwhile to say through her writing. Most importantly, Annette needed to learn to use her extended repertoire and frameworks as a resource for what she wanted to say, rather than as a substitute for having anything to say. Whilst great care needed to be taken that what Annette wrote about would be something that could be managed using the available repertoire, so that the struggle to make meaning was not self-defeating, it was perhaps the single most urgent task to bring meaning-making into her concept of what she was trying to achieve with her writing. Only then would she be in a position to exercise control *as a writer*, i.e. make decisions about what to say next, what to include and exclude, rather than simply being at the mercy of whatever emerged from the repertoire that she knew how to write. This was the precondition for her to be able to begin to respond to her teachers' current encouragement to look more critically at her writing and begin to revise it, which Annette had seemed reluctant to attempt so far.

Thus, the limitations of Annette's strategy that were inhibiting to her learning could also be linked to features of the learning environment which might be susceptible to adaptation or change in some way in order to enhance her subsequent learning. To identify such possibilities is not to detract from Annette's achievement, or from that of her teachers who so sensitively endorsed and reinforced her efforts to renegotiate status as a learner in the group over the period of the study. It is to explore how the detail of her case can be used as a 'self-correcting strategy' (Harste, Woodward and Burke, 1984) for our own thinking about the processes of teaching and learning, and as a guide to the development of practice.

CONCLUSION

My study of Annette's learning, in different ways, both endorsed and challenged the thinking that led me to identify specific conditions of the workshop approach as likely to be supportive of children's development as writers. On the one hand, Annette showed herself able not only to take the initiative but to organize a powerful and, in many respects, successful remedial programme for herself, restoring her confidence in own her ability to learn. I am convinced that the opportunity to control her writing was vital to this genuine progress, because no teacher, however expert and sensitive, could have known enough about Annette's needs in relation to the complex conjunction of circumstances in which she found herself to have been able to predict or propose a strategy so perfectly adapted to Annette's experience and existing resources as that which she devised for herself.

On the other hand, it has also provided a salutory reminder of how easy it is to take our own frames of reference for granted and forget how our curricular intentions will be transformed in practice once they have been filtered through children's own systems of meaning. Annette did not know that freedom of topic choice was supposed to be a marvellous opportunity to find her own voice and realize her own intentions in writing. She did not know that learning to write was about expressing yourself or about realizing her intentions. Writing was simply part of what she was expected to do in school. Her response to the conditions of the writing workshop reminds us of the potential for children to exercise control in ways which are counterproductive to their learning, in spite of their own best efforts and those of their teachers. Children's responses to the opportunity to control their own learning will necessarily reflect their systems of meanings, not ours.

Thus, whilst Annette's case offers encouraging evidence of how a child, who might conventionally be identified as 'having learning difficulties' could constructively make use of the opportunity to control her own learning, it also highlights the possible risks to the child if we assert the benefits of control uncritically. We need to look very carefully at the understandings and purposes which children bring to the task of learning to write, how these affect what they do, and what they might reveal about the limitations in the learning experiences and opportunities currently provided. We need to be alert, too, to children's ability to use their control to obscure from us what they do not know and cannot do, in such a way that we are denied the opportunity to question and adjust features of the experiences provided. There is clearly considerable potential here, in a busy classroom, for such inhibiting influences on children's learning to pass unnoticed, and for current achievement to be accepted as a sufficient expression of the child's abilities.

Thus, no matter what our expertise, experience or ideology, in the gap between teachers' intentions and children's responses to classroom learning experiences, there is always the potential for new, unanticipated problems to emerge. There is clearly no end to the process, no gradual ironing out of problems, no final solution. There is only a continuing process: one which requires constant vigilance on the part of teachers, a willingness not to gloss over problematic perceptions of children's learning in a well-intentioned concern to avoid deficit attributions, and to keep searching out the developmental possibilities revealed in children's responses.

Finally, Annette's case also serves as a reminder that the meanings that we find in children's responses will always, to some extent, be a projection of ourselves. Prior to writing the account, it had not occurred to me to think of motivation towards achievement as a self-protective strategy. Only as I completed the first draft did it occur to me that what I had attributed to Annette could equally, in a way, be attributed to me. What I had written was not simply an account of Annette's development but also, in important respects, of my own.

4

The Entertainer – Adrian's Story

The carpenter planes, sands, varnishes and sands again, all in *anticipation* of running the hand over the smooth surface, the pleasure to the eye of gently curving lines, the approval of friends . . . Children need to . . . receive a response to their voices, to know what comes through so that they might anticipate self-satisfaction and the *vision* of the imprint of their information on classmates or the *vision* of their work in published form. It is the forward vision, as well as the backward *vision*, that ultimately lead to major breakthroughs in a child's writing.

(Graves, 1983, p. 160)

My attention was first attracted to Adrian via a piece of writing which one of his teachers showed me, with evident excitement, at the end of a session towards the end of the Autumn term (see Figure 4.1). It was the first piece of independent writing that Adrian had produced since arriving new to the school (without previous school records) some six weeks earlier. During the first few weeks, apparently, he had refused point blank to write. Rather than press him into resistance, his teachers had invited him to record his ideas on tape. Now, at last, he had taken the initiative himself, in a session when he had the readily available help of a Section 11 teacher who was working with a group of bilingual children on the same table. I learnt from this teacher that she had helped only with spelling.

One feature of the story which made me want to follow Adrian's progress in detail was the striking contrast it revealed between Adrian's skill as a story-writer and his lack of skill in the more technical aspects of writing. The co-existence of such extremes of development was unusual, in my experience, and so made Adrian a particularly interesting choice of learner to study in detail in the workshop context. I was interested to see if and how the workshop approach might be able to support the development of both compositional and secretarial aspects of his writing. Since a marked discrepancy of development is often associated with dyslexia, observing Adrian's learning also provided an opportunity to re-examine my own thinking and presuppositions with regard to this on-going debate.

My study of Adrian extended over seven months. As with Annette, my intention was to explore what progress was achieved, what continuing difficulties were observed, and to probe the ways in which these patterns of development appeared to be bound up with the particular features of the

Figure 4.1

writing workshop that I had imagined would be supportive of children's learning. In Adrian's case, too, I also ran into difficulties in pursuing these intentions. I could see all sorts of positive ways in which the writing workshop appeared to be supporting his learning, but lacked the information and resources needed to relate this to his development. It was difficult to establish what progress had been made for a number of reasons.

Firstly, Adrian was new to the school and initially was reluctant to do any writing at all. It seemed probable, then, that any material produced early on in the study would have been more a reflection of Adrian's psychological state in adjusting to a new situation than an accurate index of his writing ability at the time. Any ostensible progress might be more a tribute to the school's ability to win Adrian's trust and harness his willing engagement in the tasks of school than a reflection of new learning.

Secondly, because of the limitations of Adrian's secretarial skills, it was impossible to ascertain with any accuracy the extent of his other writing abilities. The various pieces of writing produced were accomplished with varying degrees of support for secretarial skills (constant presence of teacher, tape recording, teacher acting as scribe, Adrian writing unaided without the presence of any teacher) which made any sort of comparison of the overall quality of the individual pieces difficult.

Thirdly, his choice of topic and genre ranged widely during the study, generating different kinds of challenges and opportunities for him to use and demonstrate his skills. It was thus difficult to know whether any new features appearing in his writing represented a development in his understandings and abilities or simply a shift to a different set of concerns, content or genre of writing already within his repertoire.

Fourthly, the more that I learnt about his compositional knowledge, the more it became evident that I did not have the resources to identify and describe what I saw as significant about his writing, let alone set this in a developmental framework by means of which to account for progression. My own experience and training in remedial work had biased me towards a linguistic rather than a literary analysis of texts. The work of Graves and Calkins offered a procedure and framework of concepts for analysing the writing process and monitoring children's development as writers, but this was more a map of significant places to look, than a vocabulary to identify and describe the significance of what might be found.

For all these reasons, the task I had set myself of probing the relationship between Adrian's progress and the specific features of the writing workshop was fraught with difficulty. Before I could attempt to make judgements about what might count as progress in relation to Adrian's writing, I had first to develop an understanding of his abilities and what he was trying to achieve through his writing, and evolve a language with which to name and describe it.

This chapter describes how, through observation, conversation and eventually collaboration with Adrian, I reached a new understanding of his extraordinarily sophisticated compositional concerns, and came to the conclusion that they were derived from experience of television watching, in much the same way as more experienced readers use their experience of reading in a writerly way to inform the creation of their individual texts. I consider how the pursuit of his project to *entertain* others through his writing was bound up with and supported by the learning conditions and opportunities provided by the writing workshop. I then return to my original intention to use my study of Adrian's learning, in part, to review my thinking about dyslexia. I explain why, on the basis of the evidence, there did not seem to be grounds for pursuing the possibility of dyslexia as a relevant factor in Adrian's spelling, even though there was undoubtedly a vital need to give systematic and carefully tailored support to his spelling development, and to ensure that his limited ability to express himself in writing did not impede his learning across the curriculum.

The analysis is structured around a key event which took place about mid-way through the study and seemed to be associated with a qualitative change in Adrian's writing activity. The event, which came about in a completely spontaneous and unplanned way, was an experience of collaborative writing with a teacher (Kieran) who happened to be covering for the class teacher's absence on that day. It was following this event that there seemed to be a perceptible shift in Adrian's perception of himself as a writer and in the quality of his engagement in writing, which significantly influenced the course of his writing activity over the subsequent term. The story explores what it was about the event that might have brought about this effect, and how it was related to the conditions of the writing workshop.

INITIAL ENCOUNTERS

In this first part of the account, I describe some of my early encounters with Adrian when I was getting to know him and beginning to get a sense of his linguistic skills and the sophistication of his compositional interests and concerns.

I have already made reference to the first piece of writing which attracted my attention to Adrian and created my first impressions of his abilities as a writer, before actually meeting him in person the following term. The appearance of the text (Figure 4.1) suggested a very inexperienced writer still struggling with letter size, letter formation and word spacing. I could not recall ever having had referred to me a child still struggling to this extent with secretarial skills at this stage of schooling. Yet, beyond the surface appearance of the text and the extraordinary house with eight chimneys, there was a most carefully crafted story opening, demonstrating the understanding and insight of an experienced author who knows how to entice his readers into a text: 'within the space of the first dozen words the reader is engaged in the process of wondering, speculating, and hypothesising, of interrogating the author through the medium of the text' (Young and Robinson, 1987, p. 159).

Adrian's carefully chosen understatement 'no ordinary pig' immediately invites speculation. So what was special about this pig? What could be 'special' about a pig? He holds our imagination in suspense by revealing just enough about the pig to generate further speculation: 'It was a magical pig'. So what were its magical powers? What would it do with them? Again, he tells us just enough to whet our appetite for what is to come: 'It could talk, it could fly, it could swim'. The repetition hints that this is but the beginning of a long list; to tell more would be to reveal too much, to spoil the surprise. Adrian stops and sums up, leaving us to speculate further on what has not so far been revealed: 'It so excellent it could do anything'.

Since the story ended here, there was no way of knowing if Adrian would have been able to continue it with equal skill. It was clear, however, that his compositional abilities by far outstripped his capacity to transcribe his ideas into writing. Indeed, the text's claim to be Chapter 1 suggests that here was a writer with substantially more ambitious intentions than he had been able so far to realize. There were also other encouraging signs of an active intelligence, working at deciphering the conventions of the written code. For example, Adrian's use of brackets to stand more concretely for the significance of space between words was an interesting solution to the problem of word separation. Although his newly started 'spelling book' indicated (as subsequent observation confirmed) that he was still struggling to spell even the most common two and three letter words, his attempt at spelling 'ennything' demonstrates his ability to make connections between his existing knowledge of sound–symbol relationships and the sound in an unfamiliar word he was trying to spell.

When I met Adrian in person early in the Spring term, he was enthusiastically planning his next story. This, he told me, was to be about an invasion of the earth by 'a malevolent adversary'. He enlisted my help (and that of everybody else seated around the table) in deciding whether the 'adversary' should be the Daleks or some giant ants. He had a large, illustrated *Dr. Who* book which he kept referring to during the discussion, showing me and others his favourite bits. After much discussion, he eventually settled on the Daleks, claiming that he would be able to use his *Dr Who* book for help with spelling. He then began work simultaneously on the writing and on a picture, using the picture to record, explore and help to remember his ideas, while he laboured over transcribing them into text (see Figure 4.2).

Since I was present throughout the time that this story was being conceived and written, I was able to observe the time and intense effort required for Adrian to produce just a few sentences. Every letter of every word was painstakingly thought out and recorded individually, sometimes with a noticeable lapse of time between writing the individual letters of one word, which helped to shed light on the unevenness of his writing and spacing. Adrian refused his teacher's suggestion not to worry too much about spelling initially, in order to concentrate first on getting the ideas down. He was afraid, he told me, that we would not be able to read back what he had written afterwards.

The drawing played a vital part in sustaining this process, both as a source of relief and renewed energy. It was a story in a picture. Each time Adrian went back to it, new things happened: people threatened or attacked one another or yelled for help. Adrian worked out the details of what would happen, and had such fun with his ideas that it did not seem, at the time, to matter whether or not they would ever be written.

What was most striking, though, in all this activity was the contrast between the ideas rehearsed orally and those which eventually found their way into his story. This second story was far more complex in concept than the earlier one, perhaps brought about by the shift in genre and Adrian's growing confidence. It seemed to be designed to appeal to a more sophisticated audience. The choice of location in time was particularly complex and intriguing: writing about the present (or possibly the immediate future) as if it were an historic event, viewed from some undefined vantage point in the future (as, say, in *Planet of the Apes*).

Figure 4.2

Adrian put much thought into the details of the plot: not just who the 'adversary' should be but whether to state precisely where on Earth the Daleks invaded, and if so whether this should be Britain or elsewhere. The eventual choice of a far-off location (Armenia) for the invasion created the opportunity to send the British army in to the rescue (Armenia was in the news at the time) and then to heighten tension and fear of impending doom by showing that the British army seemed unable to make much impact on the Daleks: 'I am afared to tell you the Daleks were winning.'

Though as much skill was demonstrated in this text as in the previous one in guiding the reader into the story, the quality and quantity of what he eventually produced (which took several sessions) was undoubtedly a poor indication of the ideas he would have been capable of developing in writing, had he not been impeded by his secretarial skills. Whereas in the earlier story, I only guessed that Adrian knew how the story would evolve if he had had the skills to complete it, in this case I knew that he had already worked out the details of his plot in advance, because he had rehearsed them in his drawing. Of course, having imaginative ideas is not the same as knowing how to embody them in a text. Nevertheless, the limited evidence of Adrian's unaided production so far suggested that he did, in fact, know a great deal about crafting text, that what was impeding him from demonstrating this was his limited facility with spelling and handwriting.

A week later, he told me he was planning 'the sequel' in which Dr. Who would come to save Armenia. It would be called 'Dr Who and the awesome fighting machine'. However, the text was never written. Soon after, Adrian got into a fight in the playground and was excluded. He did not return to school again until after half term. With this news, his earlier choice of theme, in writing about a 'malevolent adversary' took on a new significance. Indeed, he pursued the 'adversarial' theme in a new form on his return, this time recording his ideas on tape. It was a play about playtime, which started off in the playground and ended up in a land below the playground where he found himself fighting off giant tarantulas by making vibrations using rapping (this was the verbal explanation, almost verbatim, which Adrian gave me as he explained his tape to me). The parallel between the theme of his story and his own recent experience leading to exclusion suggested to me that Adrian understood intuitively one of the key functions of writing: namely, the part that it can play in making sense of and coming to terms with experience, particularly with problems in one's life.

At a more conscious level, this piece seems to have suggested to Adrian that he could use his ideas and his writing as a bridge with other children, given that he found it difficult to establish relationships by more informal means. When I went to find him, he was listening to his recording, eyes alight with satisfaction and amusement not just in appreciation of his own ideas but in anticipation of how they would be received by others.

In this case, his efforts were well-rewarded. At the end of the session, during sharing time, he had the opportunity to play the first part of the tape to the rest of the class. The other children gave it their full attention, laughing and responding to the voices and effects. Adrian laughed with them and appeared to be very satisfied with their reaction.

The following week provided further insight into the originality of his ideas and his linguistic competence in communicating them, as he worked on illustrations for the book he was making arising from the transcribed tape. His first drawing, he told me, was a 'carpet-eye view' of Linda telling the children that it was playtime (the point at which his playtime story started). He had the words coming out of her mouth, and was debating how to represent visually the fact that she was shouting. He pointed out that 'Miss has got x-ray vision because she's looking one way but knows what is going on behind her back'. The book was to be called 'Day Dream

Adventure', he said, because 'that's what I was doing when the adventure happened'.

He seemed to have settled down again in school and continued to give energy and commitment to his writing, in spite of his acute difficulties in actually putting his ideas down on paper. I had been wondering why, given his imagination and evident linguistic abilities, he seemed to experience so little frustration when, one day, there was a sudden outburst of anger and self-denigration. Announcing that he wanted to re-write the earlier piece on the Daleks' invasion, he screwed up the original, and threw it in the waste bin with an elaborate display of disgust. Rescuing it (with his permission), I asked him what was wrong with it. He claimed that it was rubbish. 'My mum wouldn't be very proud of that', he declared, 'I want to do it better. I can do it better'.

Remembering the pleasure he had shown with the ideas while the piece was being written, I was surprised at this repudiation. Questioning Linda about it, I learnt that there was some pressure from home which led him now to focus on the deficiencies, whereas previously he had considered it marvellously inventive. Linda showed me a piece of writing which he had done at home (while excluded). His mother had corrected it, obviously with the best of intentions, by crossing out words which were not written in standard spelling and writing the correct spelling over the top. Given the number of errors, the page of writing was almost totally obliterated, yet this piece of writing looked to me like his most extended and ambitious story so far.

It was at this point that Kieran, a teacher on permanent supply at the school and who happened to be working in the class at the time, stepped in. Sensing, perhaps, that Adrian's confidence was shaken and that he might need some extra help to get going again, Kieran began talking Adrian through what he planned to write for his next story and writing the ideas down for him. Out of this chance initiative, a collaborative writing experience developed which, I later realized, prompted a significant change in Adrian's writing activity.

UNTAPPED RESOURCES?

Initially, Kieran simply supported a discussion on the table where Adrian was sitting to establish an outline of the story. Adrian decided to change the plot line from the original Dalek story, to make it about a rescue of someone kidnapped by the Daleks. In the new version, Adrian himself was to be the hero rescuer, fearlessly outwitting the Daleks alongside Dr. Who. Another new idea was to include real, famous people as the kidnappees, presumably to add to the interest and quasi-veracity to the story. The question was who? Eventually, amidst much laughter, argument and jeers, Michael Jackson and Kylie Minogue were selected.

While the rest of the class got on with their writing, Kieran gave his complete attention to Adrian. To start with, he merely wrote at Adrian's dictation, but eventually the two of them began to discuss and collaborate jointly in the making of the story. Initially, I thought that I probably would not be able to use the extraordinary story which resulted (Figure 4.3) as part of the data for this study, since I only observed this collaborative process from a distance and so clearly cannot identify with any certainty the contribution which Adrian made to the construction of the story.

It happened in 1989 when the Daleks invaded the Earth. The famous Michael Jackson and Kylie Minogue had been kidnapped. One day Adrian was reading an article and he read it out loud to Yalkin. And it read:

> The famous Michael Jackson and Kylie Minogue have been kidnapped. Will somebody please volunteer to rescue them?

At that time, thousands of millions of miles away in space, Doctor Who was reading the same newspaper, and saw the same article and read it out to Ace. At that time Doctor Who just knew that Adrian the Great and Yalkin the Superb were going to rescue Michael Jackson and Kylie Minogue. So he came down in his tardis and appeared in their living room.

"Ah, Adrian," said Doctor Who. Meanwhile Ace was busy talking to Yalkin.

But still meanwhile the Daleks were planning. Distemper said, "What happens if the Doctor doesn't come? What will we do with these?"
The Emperor Dalek said, "We will ex-ter-min-ate them."
So Distemper said, "And if they do come?"
"We will ex-ter-min-ate the Doctor, and then we will ex-ter-min-ate these two. And then we will eliminate the whole of the universe."
Michael Jackson said, "Blimey, is that all you're going to do?"
Distemper said, "Shut up, or we'll exterminate you."
So Kylie said, "That's a nice attitude."
"And you shut up as well," said Distemper, "or I'll lose my temper."
"Now I see why they call you Distemper," said Michael Jackson.
"Shut up, I told you!"

Meanwhile, back in Adrian's house the Doctor and Adrian were thinking how to rescue them. Anthony and his friends went over to Afia's house, and Afia suggested we set our own trap. Yalkin said, "But how do we set our own trap?"
Anthony said, "Good question."
And the Doctor said, "Quite easy really."
So the Doctor told them the plan.

Meanwhile the Daleks were thinking of their own plan. Distemper said, "How do we get rid of the Doctor?"
And Savros said, "When he comes to rescue them, we'll all stand back, and see that x there, when he steps on that to rescue them, we'll jump out and blast them!"

Back in Adrian's house, the Doctor said, "Let's go to your little base place."
So Adrian said, "Yalkin, press the special button. You and Ace go in your Super-Wackid car, me and the Doctor will go in the other garage.

Figure 4.3

Doctor, we'll go in the firecracker."

And the Doctor said, "Is it fast?"
"It's so fast the tyres will leave fire behind on the road."
"But won't that burn up our car following behind?" asked Yalkin.
"No. You've got special rubber-helium-gas-telium tyres."
And Afia said, "You must have them too then."

Adrian pressed the super button in the car, and went so fast that Yalkin had to call the fire-brigade, and if you want to know how many fire engines there was, there was 200 of them, because the car went so fast.

Adrian and the Doctor were wearing cross seat belts, so one went one way and one went the other, and they were wearing crash helmets, and Adrian said, "I told you it goes fast."

The Doctor said, "You weren't kidding. But how do we know where the Daleks' base is?"

Adrian stopped dead in his tracks, and made an enormous congestion which was even bigger than the M1's congestions. Adrian thought to himself, "Why are we going so fast when we don't know where the base is?"

In Yalkin's car, Yalkin said, "I wonder why they stopped."
Afia said, "They probably don't even know where they're going."
The Doctor got out of the car, and went over to Yalkin's car and said, "Ace, pass me your cassette player."

Afia said, "Is this the time to have a party?"
"I want to see the Daleks on the radar screen," said the Doctor.
And Afia said, "It's only a cassette player. Let's not get flash with ourselves now."

The Doctor said, "Oh, be quiet. Ace, you can see them on the radar screen?"

"No, Doctor, I can't."
"Well, look harder." And the Doctor just noticed something. "They are there, but we can't see them."

Afia said, "I'll believe that when I see it."
And just then, they did see it; a 22,000 feet megawatt Dalek standing straight in front of them.

And Afia said, "I still don't believe it."
And just then the Dalek said, "Well, you'd better believe it."
Afia said, "I still don't believe it." But Afia thought to herself a wicked plan. She said, "Well I'd have to see Michael Jackson and Kylie Minogue before I believe it."

So the Dalek took them there, and Distemper said, "Don't stand on that x or you'll be x-ecuted."

And the Doctor said, "Why don't you stand on it, Distemper, and show us what you mean."

"Good idea," said Distemper.
So Distemper stood on it. And Savros said, "Blast it."
"Aaaarrghh" screamed Distemper.
And the Doctor said, "Good one, Afia."
And Afia said, "What d'you mean, good one?"
Adrian said to the Doctor, "Looks like she's lost her brains."
"Oh well," said the Doctor, "It was fun while it lasted."
"What do you mean," said Afia.
    Adrian said, "Yes. Perhaps you were right, I did enjoy being

Figure 4.3

chased by the Daleks."

"Oh Adrian," said Ace, "Can you show me how you build them cars?"

Just at that moment Michael Jackson said, "Get us untied!"

And Yalkin said, "Come on, let's leave them here."

"You can't do that!"

"Want a bet?" said Yalkin, "I never liked their singing anyway. Quick! Look, there's a Dalek. One-nil, one-nil."

"You've had enough time to talk, you are just buying time," said Savros.

"Just one more minute, please," said the Doctor.

"10 ...20 ...50 ...60; time's up."

"Oh, just give us another quarter of an hour," said the Doctor.

"Very well."

"Quick, Ace, hand me your cassette player. If we can just reverse the pleromality, then we can make the electric reverse, then if the brown wire touches the white wire, which touches the satellite, which sends the satellite off control, which should, when the Daleks shoot us, reverse their ray like a mirror, which, when they're blown up, the shock of that will send their radio transistors to their base, which, if it wrecks their other transistors will blow their ship up, which should make their other ship land, and then when the Mother ship lands, will destroy that with another of Afia's brilliant plans, which should blow the Mother ship up, which should make the Dad ship land, then that machine that I was going to build will wipe out the Daddy ship."

Afia said, "But supposing there's an Uncle ship, that makes the granny ship land, that makes the grandaddy ship land ..."

"Well I suppose there's no time to waste about silly comments."

So when the Daddy ship landed, it was lucky for us that we has our machine ready built, and already in waiting; and then we blew them sky high, just like that. So Michael Jackson and Kylie Minogue went back to their singing, and Adrian and Yalkin were famous detectives and brilliant technologists. Afia was known as plain Afia Super Brain, just like on Neighbours, and me and Yalkin were known as Yalkin the Superb and Adrian the Great. Then we started partying. Life went on, as it always does, and that's really the end of the story, to be honest.

Figure 4.3

This was frustrating because I was convinced that the qualities which impressed me in the writing were not simply due to the teacher's contribution. They were qualities which I recognized from Adrian's linguistic repertoire, even though they had never previously found their way into a text. They had a definite feel of Adrian about them, rather than the feel of an adult helping to shape the text. It is often difficult to judge the extent of one's own input, but Kieran commented particularly on the humour and unusual inventiveness which Adrian had displayed during the course of their work together.

Eventually, I found a way to use the text that did not depend upon precise knowledge of Adrian's personal contribution. I used it to help explore and substantiate an emerging thesis about the significance of this event in confirming Adrian as a writer. Subsequent events over the following term led me to conclude that what Kieran had done through this experience was not just to remove the impediment presented by Adrian's limited secretarial skills, and so free him to give full rein to his creative resources. He had also tapped a set of resources which Adrian already had, but had not yet realized that he could use, or realized how to use, in the context of school writing. It was when Adrian commented, one day much later on, that television was a major source of ideas for his writing that it occurred to me that he was not simply referring to plot or characters (e.g. Dr. Who), but to *television literacy* as the source of *compositional knowledge*. What had happened, perhaps, in the experience with Kieran, was that Adrian had suddenly seen the legitimacy and relevance of this out-of-school knowledge for in-school writing.

Before meeting Adrian, I would probably have gone along with many commentators on children's writing who regard television as having a deadening influence on children's creativity. Graves (1983), for instance, refers disparagingly to 'yesterday's stale TV plot', which may provide a necessary springboard for some children to move into creative writing, but the aim should be to encourage children to move on as quickly as possible to more personally meaningful and original topics for their writing. However, Adrian demonstrated the possibility for using television resources in a constructive and creative way, much as more literate writers use their experience of reading books:

> in order to learn to write we must learn to read, but, we must learn to read in the role of the writer. That is, during the act of reading, the processes of reading and writing must lose their separate identities and be fused in the mind of the reader into a single act: the reader must become the writer. In this way ... the act of reading becomes a composing process.
>
> (Young and Robinson, 1987, p. 153)

Adrian had learned to *watch* in the role of the writer. He had a vast fund of ideas, from endless television watching, as a result of studying very carefully how effects that particularly held his attention, or that amused and entertained him, were achieved. These were not borrowed plots, but amusing verbal sequences, repartee, puns and ways of wrong-footing audience expectations which he understood and appreciated himself in his favourite programmes, and now, having received the go-ahead from Kieran, began to try to reproduce in his writing.

Although I could not be certain, then, what contribution Adrian made to the text he and Kieran produced together, I could use the text to explore the thesis that Adrian *could* have derived the knowledge and understandings that were necessary in order to achieve the qualities it revealed through watching television. I chose a particular television programme (*The Hitchhikers' Guide to the Galaxy*) which, it occurred to me, bore a resemblance in genre and humour to their text. I then studied this closely, alongside the text, attempting to identify and describe similarities in textual devices used.

COMPARING WRITTEN TEXT AND TELEVISION TEXT

Adrian's story has a complex opening structure, with three successive scenes happening in simultaneous time which introduce the overall plot. This is a device commonly used in television and film, where the audience needs to be introduced simultaneously to different dimensions of the plot. The first two scenes are introduced 'straight', leading us to anticipate an adventure story in the science fiction/fantasy/adventure genre of the *Dr. Who* series. The third however, deliberately disrupts our expectations, alerting us to the writer's intention also to parody the genre (see Figure 4.3).

```
    But still meanwhile the Daleks were planning. Distemper said, "What
happens if the Doctor doesn't come? What will we do with these?"
    The Emperor Dalek said, "We will ex-ter-min-ate them."
    So Distemper said, "And if they do come?"
    "We will ex-ter-min-ate the Doctor, and then we will ex-ter-min-
ate these two. And then we will eliminate the whole of the universe."
    Michael Jackson said, "Blimey, is that all you're going to do?"
    Distemper said, "Shut up, or we'll exterminate you."
    So Kylie said, "That's a nice attitude."
    "And you shut up as well," said Distemper, "or I'll lose my temper."
    "Now I see why they call you Distemper," said Michael Jackson.
    "Shut up, I told you!"
```

The Daleks' powers of extermination, supposedly so terrifying in the original, become a source of entertainment in Adrian's version. The absurd overstatement of their threat to 'ex-ter-mi-nate the whole universe' invites ridicule rather than fear ('Blimey, is that all you're going to do?'). We realize that these dangerous Daleks are in fact bumbling idiots and the fun of the story is going to be to see how easily, for all their technological weaponry and threats, they can be taken in and outwitted by the team of superheroes.

A similar juxtaposition of imminent personal danger, satirical humour and ridicule of the all-powerful captors is found in *The Hitchhikers' Guide*. For example, as an enormous and terrifying alien emerges roaring from the shadows, this exchange takes place between the two hitchhikers:

What on earth is it?
If we're lucky it's a Vogon guard come to throw us into space.
And if we're unlucky?
The Vogon captain may want to read us some of his poetry first.

In Adrian's story, as in the *Hitchhikers' Guide* quasi-authenticity is claimed for the story-as-science-fiction by creating a specialist made-up vocabulary of high-tech-sounding words to dazzle and intrigue the audience (e.g. 'Superwackid car', 'rubber-helium-gas-telium tyres', 'reverse the pleromality' in Adrian's; 'pan-galactic gargle blaster', 'electronic sub-ether device', 'Matta transference beam', 'Bamberweeny 57 submeson brain' in the *Hitchhikers' Guide*).

Ridiculously complicated, unintelligible quasi-scientific instructions and explanations presented as comprehensible communication are another humorous feature. For example, in Adrian's story, there is a passage which begins:

> Quick, Ace, hand me your cassette player . . . If we can just reverse the pleromality, then we can make the electric reverse, then if the brown wire touched the white wire, which touches the satellite, which sends the satellite off control, which should, when the Daleks shoot us, reverse their ray like a mirror, which. . . .

This parallels a similar moment of crisis and panic in the *Hitchhikers' Guide*, when missiles are about to hit the spaceship. Trillion has a sudden flash of inspiration:

> Zephod, do you think we could stabilize in X zero zero five four seven if we split our flight path tangentially across the semi effect of nine CX and seven eighths with a five degree inertia connection?

Both in Adrian's writing and in the *Hitchhikers' Guide* we find attempts to create effect through extravagant, often absurd, comparisons and analogies. Adrian later referred to this technique as his 'calculations', claiming that he 'always' found ways to include these in his writing. What he was referring to was a conscious intention to emphasize the size, distance, weight, and other characteristics of people or objects by expressing these in numerical or metaphorical terms. Thus, for example, in this story, we meet Dr. Who reading the paper 'thousands of millions of miles away in space', a '20,000 feet megawatt Dalek', and a car which goes so fast that the tyres 'leave fire behind on the road'. Indeed, on one occasion, the car 'went so fast' that not only did Yalkin have to call the fire brigade but it required 200 fire engines to quell the flames.

The *Hitchhikers' Guide* exploits similar numerical extravagances, but also specializes in invoking more unexpected images for comparison:

> Drinking a Pan Galactic gargle blaster is like having your brains smashed out with a slice of lemon . . . wrapped around a large gold brick.

> You should never drink more than two Pan Galactic gargle blasters unless you are a thirty megaton elephant with bronchial pneumonia.

In Adrian's story, as in the *Hitchhikers' Guide*, it is not just the villains who are made targets for humour and parody. Just as we have been invited to gasp with admiration at the speed of the 'firecracker' car, the text turns on the extravagant boastings of its superheroes revealing that, in spite of all this speed, they do not actually know where they are going.

> Adrian stopped dead in his tracks, and made an enormous congestion which was even bigger than the M1's congestions. Adrian thought to himself 'Why are we going so fast when we don't even know where the base is?'

This ability of the text to play with its own conventions and, by that means, confound our expectations is also at the heart of the humour of the *Hitchhikers' Guide*. For example, with much pomp and ceremony, the electronic book takes us back:

> Far back in the mists of ancient time, in the great and glorious days of the former Galactic Empire, life was wild, rich and largely tax free. Mighty starships plied their way between exotic suns, seeking adventure and reward amongst the furthest reaches of Galactic space. In those days spirits were brave, the stakes were high, men were real men, women were real women, and small furry creatures from Alpha Centauri were real small furry creatures from Alpha Centauri.

Both texts, then, show a similar ability to engage in a constant process of self-monitoring, to recognize the potential for play with meanings, and to divert the text to explore them in ways which amusingly (or sometimes tiresomely) disrupt our expectations.

Moreover, the presence of stereotypical characters who are boring, conventional, or not very bright finding themselves in highly unfamiliar or problematic situations creates all sorts of amusing possibilities for misunderstanding and miscommunication because they lack information which others take for granted. In Adrian's story, Afia appears to play this role:

> The Doctor . . . said 'Ace, pass me your cassette player.'
> Afia said, 'Is this the time to have a party?'
> 'I want to see the Daleks on the radar screen' said the Doctor.
> And Afia said, 'It's only a cassette player. Let's not get flash with ourselves now.'
> The Doctor said, 'Oh be quiet'.

whereas in the *Hitchhikers' Guide*, it is played by Arthur Dent:

> 'How did we get here?'
> 'We hitched a lift.'
> 'Hitched a lift? Are you trying to tell me that we stuck our thumbs out and some green bug-eyed monster stuck his head out and said hi fellas hop right in I can take you as far as the Basingstoke roundabout?'
> 'Well, the thumb's an electronic sub-ether signalling device, and the roundabout's at Barnard Star six light years away, but otherwise, that's more or less right.'
> 'And the bug-eyed monster. . . ?'
> 'Is green . . . yes!'

The presence of this character also sets up expectations which allow for interesting plot twists when it is the 'dim' or 'innocent' one who unexpectedly comes up with the idea which saves the day. Thus in the *Hitchhikers' Guide* it is Arthur Dent who decides to press the switch which moves the spaceship into infinite improbability drive and thus saves it from certain destruction by on-coming missiles. In Adrian's story, it is Afia who tricks the Daleks into taking them to the base.

Self-parody and disruption of conventional meanings continues in Adrian's story as, with yet another twist of the plot, the question is suddenly raised as to whether anyone actually wants to rescue Michael Jackson and Kylie Minogue, or whether it might not be in everyone's interests to leave them there ('I never liked their singing anyway'). Suddenly we are reminded of the duplicity of the text which has commanded our support for the rescuers, and which is now inviting us to raise the question of whether the rescue was actually worth the trouble in the first place.

We have now seen that it is possible to establish a number of points of similarity between the two texts which would appear to endorse the possibility that Adrian *could* have developed his understanding of these, to paraphrase Smith (1983), by watching in the role of the writer. It would seem to be plausible, then, that the qualitative change which I sensed in Adrian's writing activity, at about the mid-point of the study, came about not only as a result of having the support and collaboration of an appreciative partner who helped to engage Adrian's linguistic and compositional skills at a more sophisticated level, but also as a result of realizing, through this experience, that he could legitimately draw on his resources derived from television-watching as an aid to his writing. Of course, the nature of this change, and the significance of the collaborative experience in bringing it about, only became apparent gradually over the course of the following term. Nevertheless, two qualitative changes did occur immediately, indicating a new authority and sense of purpose that Adrian was bringing to his writing. The first was to enlist my help as his scribe; the second was to shift his writing almost exclusively into dialogue form.

It seemed to occur to Adrian at this point that my regular presence in the classroom could be used to make the kind of opportunity which Kieran had provided available to him on a more regular basis. His teachers agreed on condition that he undertook to do at least part of the writing himself during each lesson. Our collaboration served both our interests in different ways. I helped him by scribing, typing and providing a sounding board for his writing. He helped me by articulating his thinking at each stage and increasingly becoming interested in my research. Our collaboration convinced me that Adrian was not only aware, at a conscious and explicit level, of the effect he was aiming to create through his writing but was also beginning to evolve his own language and concepts to articulate the decision-making involved in his writing process. Our discussions gave me new insights into his abilities by giving me access to the intention behind the words and ideas, by enabling me to share ideas that were entertained and problems that were grappled with but which never, to my knowledge, found their way into a particular text. They also created a situation in which Adrian felt comfortable, and so free, to offer spontaneous comments about himself, about his writing, and about his previous experience of writing. These additional sources of information meant that I could be much less tentative about asserting what I increasingly felt (though still lacked the concepts to describe) were the exceptional linguistic abilities and understandings of this child.

SCENES IN THE MIND

> It is ultimately impossible to convey a musical composition or pictorial image adequately in words ... nor is there any really adequate verbal substitute for even the simplest gesture in human behaviour.
>
> (Volosinov, 1973, p. 15)

Adrian's 'Super S' story started off in conventional narrative form, with Linda scribing, during a wet playtime immediately before writing workshop (see Figure 4.4). The two opening paragraphs (scribed by his teacher) were carefully crafted, drawing the reader into the story, creating a sense of anticipation and beginning to construct the details of the fictional world we were being invited to share. The story opens with a sense of calm before the storm. The reader knows that, in spite of what is being said, something is about to happen. But where are we? Who are these people? What is going to happen? Suddenly, the alarm goes, and we realize there is an emergency of some kind. However, we have to wait now in suspense to find out what will happen. Having captured our interest, Adrian steps outside the immediate happenings to give us the background information that provide the context for the the story. We discover that the time is the future, and the players are Adrian's class in the future: an interesting new dimension which would doubtless appeal to the rest of the class. Adrian anticipates our question of how we and the world look now, in the future, and gives us some insights into the impact of progress by means of his 'calculations' ('we have boats propelled a thousand times faster than a Concorde's engine').

At the base, everybody was bored. And Manni said, "Nothing ever happens here. I'm bored of it." suddenly just then 'Ding' went the alarm. "Ha," said Sofia, "Now something's happening."

The 'Super S' Company is the whole of Liz's class, when they're grown up. We are now in the year 2000, the start of the 21st century. The world has changed lots. We have machines that can go faster than sound, faster than the speed of light, and we have boats propelled a thousand times faster than a Concorde's engine.

Figure 4.4

At this point, Linda had left Adrian to continue on his own. After some time without any sign of activity, Adrian wrote six words and then called me over. He explained that he had been stuck because he could not see how to find a way of getting back naturally into the story after the diversion needed to fill in the background. The solution which he had come up with, and wanted to test out on me, was to make the alarm ring again. He had written 'Ding' They ran to their cars' (see Figure 4.5). This use of repetition did indeed serve to bring the reader neatly back into the story. Then, by continuing the narrative, at least briefly, Adrian was able to establish himself as the implied leader of the company (class group), responding to instructions from 'Sir'.

However, it seemed that a conventional narrative was not what Adrian

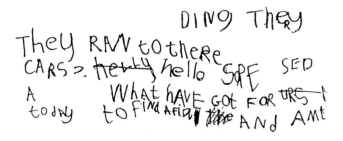

Figure 4.5

was aspiring to in this case. His aim, it gradually emerged, was to make people feel that they were actually *there* in the midst of the action, and his way of trying to create that experience was to write the story entirely through dialogue. Writing a story in dialogue, however, presented new challenges. Next I found him trying to work out how to indicate to an audience who was speaking without having to state 'so-and-so said' each time, which would be boring, as well as getting in the way of people's sense of being there. Adrian experimented with two solutions. The first, he explained to me, was to use 'Yes' plus the name of an individual tagged on to the end of the previous speaker, to indicate who was being invited to speak next (see Figure 4.6). The second was to indicate retrospectively who had spoken, by

---

"To find Afia and Amjad. Find their murderers!"
"Does it include lots of people?"
"Good question. Yes. It involves the Archbishop Gang. Yes, Manni?"
"Weren't they the ones who helped capture Terry Waite?"
"Yes, indeed they were. They capture famous people too often. So that's why they've captured Afia and Amjad. Yes, Nazral?"

Figure 4.6

attaching their name to the end of the reply. Thus someone shouts 'No!' and we learn who did the shouting when (presumably) Adrian responds 'Why not, Yalkin?' (see Figure 4.7). Satisfied with his solution, Adrian shifted his writing from this point in the story almost entirely into dialogue form.

While encouraging and appreciating his ideas, his teachers made repeated attempts to dissuade him from this project throughout the term on the grounds

```
"Let's get going?"
"No!"
"Why not, Yalkin?"
"Because it might be a trap."
```

Figure 4.7

that dialogue on its own left out essential narrative ingredients that were needed if the audience was to follow what was happening. However, Adrian would not be dissuaded. Indeed, he expressed frustration on occasions throughout the term that 'nobody understood' what he was trying to achieve with his writing. I certainly had to question him closely sometimes, in scribing his work, to make sense of exactly what was supposed to be happening. It seemed initially that in his excitement for the ideas, Adrian was failing to take sufficient account of the needs of his audience. For instance, he left the audience to deduce for themselves the arrival of the 'Archbishop Gang', and how they had managed to sneak up on the Super S company unnoticed. He made no attempt to clarify, from a confusion of voices, who was saying what and what was going on when fighting first broke out (see Figure 4.8). 'Oh look there's the Incredible Hulk' was meant to be the old, old trick of distracting attention, but who shouts it (Adrian presumably)? Who attacks who and what exactly happens? More contextual detail was needed if the audience was to be able to savour the excitement that Adrian intended.

```
"Oh yeh?"
"Who said that?"
"I did. Now stick up your hands."
"I tried to warn you."
"I suppose you did, didn't you, Yalkin?"
"SHUT UP, I SAID!"
"Who are you?"
"Never mind that now."
"Oh, you're the Archbishop Gang."
"I SAID SHUT UP!"
"OH LOOK THERE'S THE INCREDIBLE HULK!"
"Where? Where? Where?"
Zot ZOT! PAM! AAAAHH! CRACK!
```

Figure 4.8

However, the idea that Adrian, in an excess of enthusiasm, might be giving insufficient thought to his audience's needs was at odds with the evidence that *all* Adrian's compositional concerns during this period were focused on making his meaning clear to his audience. He was continually thinking about how to create particular effects in dialogue, with the emphasis on how to ensure that the ideas came across to an audience in the way that he intended. He expressed frustration that 'words aren't good enough' for the meanings that he was trying to convey.

On one occasion, pressed to explain what he meant, he gave a number of examples. He made the sound of a motorbike going round a corner and claimed that there was no word for this sound. There was no word to express what sound people make when they go into a huddle and all you can hear is whispering (some sort of sound like 'psspsspsspss'). Writing down the words someone spoke does not tell you how they were spoken (whether they were shouted, spoken or whispered for instance), and Adrian would constantly try to negotiate different ways of presenting the words in dialogue to convey his effect (e.g. using capital letters to indicate shouting). Similarly, he was aware that much of the meaning of spoken language (e.g. sarcasm, irony) is conveyed through intonation patterns, yet these do not come through when dialogue is written rather than spoken.

On another occasion, he rehearsed aloud an amusing idea he wanted to use but was unsure how to get across what was amusing about it in writing. The line was:

'Gosh, that's amazing, fantastic . . . . wowee! . . . . what is it?'

This was very similar to the 'about-face' in the Dr. Who story, when Dr. Who and Adrian set off somewhere at phenomenal speed in the 'Super-Wackid car', only to discover a moment later that they do not know where they are going. The words were 'not good enough', it seems, because Adrian could see that the joke involved many layers of understanding that were implied rather than made explicit in what was said.

Was the problem that, in spite of the sophistication of Adrian's compositional interests, he was simply misunderstanding the function of dialogue, and how it needs to be supported by surrounding narrative detail? Or was he trying to achieve something else that only appeared deficient because it was being measured against the wrong conventional criteria? For instance, if Adrian was implicitly assuming an eventual comic-book format for his writing, then the dialogue which he produced would have been perfectly sufficient to function as an accompaniment to pictures.

At first, when Adrian told me that he got his ideas from television ('mixed with ideas in my mind'), I felt slightly disappointed, as if this somehow detracted from the qualities that had impressed me. Gradually, however, as I attempted to understand the significance of his focus on dialogue-writing, I began to form a very different sense of what 'getting ideas from television' might mean. I began to see the possibility that his work could, perhaps, legitimately be understood as a kind of script (minus the stage directions): a way of providing for others a means of recreating through dialogue and action the vivid scenes which he conjured up in his mind.

On television, of course, the only language used is in spoken form. It seemed to me, with hindsight, that once Adrian had realized that it was legitimate to draw on the resources he had accumulated from watching television in his writing in school, he took this idea a stage further. Instead of embodying ideas which had their source in television programmes into a narrative, as he had done with Kieran, he was now trying to write directly from the visual medium of television, using dialogue in the way that it functions in a television story, and trying to do justice, through this dialogue, to the amusing scenes that he conjured up in his mind.

Alongside Adrian's own comments ('my mind is like a sampling machine'), I eventually deduced this extraordinarily ambitious project from the content and form of Adrian's writing and from the overall focus of his compositional concerns during this period. Adrian referred to what he was writing as an 'adventure story', claiming that what was distinctive about his work (compared to that of other children) was that he wrote 'mad stories'. This I took to be a reference to his conscious attempts to play with language, and with his audience expectations, to inject humour, interest and suspense into the story. 'The virtuous writer recognises the artifice of all writing and proceeds to make play with it (Selden, 1985, p. 74, with reference to the work of Roland Barthes). For example, having played the 'action' fairly straight as an adventure story up to the point of confrontation with the Archbishop Gang, Adrian suddenly inserts a sequence which plays humorously with the literal and implied meanings of the language of 'threat' (see Figure 4.9).

```
"STOP!"
"STOP OR WE'LL RELEASE THE BEAGLE BUGS ...."
"OOOOOOH NO!"
"I said I'll release them."
"And I said OOOOOOOOH no!"
"Parrot!"
"Stop it Yalkin or you'll cost us our lives!"
"Are they worth living?"
"STOP! STOP! STOP! STOP ...."
"That's no good. If the Archbishop Gang were about to jump in
n o w ...."
```

Figure 4.9

Adrian-the-leader intervenes to reassert the 'straight' line of the plot ('Stop it Yalkin or you'll cost us our lives') but Yalkin refuses to be drawn in, continuing to play with meanings and parody Adrian's attempts to present their situation as one of fatal danger. Suddenly, the action is brought to a complete halt ('STOP! STOP! STOP! STOP') and we discover, in an unexpected twist of plot, that the confrontation with the Archbishop Gang has been merely a simulation (Adrian's own word). If we (as readers) have taken it for 'real' action (within the fiction-presented-as-real) we have been taken in. It was an illusion (again Adrian's word), designed to prepare Super S company for what might happen if the Archbishop Gang really did spring in on them.

All this had to be explained to me in some detail by Adrian, and is by no means made explicit through the dialogue, although the dialogue makes sense once Adrian's meanings have been clarified. It was a complex idea which functioned to enhance the seeming reality of the fictional world Adrian was inviting his audience to inhabit. By constructing a fiction within a fiction, the reality of the original fiction appears to be confirmed.

The 'Boss' appears and starts to complain about the general shambles, at which point the Archbishop Gang really does arrive, although Adrian-in-the-story assumes that this is yet another simulation (see Figure 4.10). The plot

```
CRASH!
"Very good, Sir. But that's not really them."
"Anthony . . . That's not an illusion . . . ."
Ah! Ah! Ah! Ah! Ah! Ah! Ah! Ah!

"Where's Wai Kit?"
"Never mind."
"I said, give us Wai Kit back."
```

Figure 4.10

collapses into slapstick as a fight ensues, most of the company are over-powered by the Archbishop Gang, and one of their number (Wai Kit) is mysteriously spirited away. Amusing gags are introduced as Adrian and others try various ruses in order to escape against impossible odds ('well, we've got to be going . . .) but fail and are marched on to the spaceship. The plot twists again as we discover, through a series of well-managed rapid exchanges that the Gang do not know how to fly the spaceship. Meanwhile, the people who do know how to fly it are tied up and helpless (see Figure 4.11).

```
"Didn't you know the safety rules?"
"What safety rules?"
"That when flying a spaceship . . ."
"WATCH OUT!!"
"What happens when you lose orbit?"
"You might have a nasty spaceship accident."
"Well, untie them then!"
"I think you'd better untie them very fast!"
```

Figure 4.11

In the exchanges which follow, Adrian perhaps comes closest to his aim of enabling readers to feel as if they are actually 'there' in the midst of the action. The dialogue conveys with considerable skill the panic of the Gang leaders as they lose control of the spaceship, yell instructions to one another and pre-pare to crash (see Figure 4.12). As well as being suspenseful, the panic is also intended to be humorous: their reaction to the crisis symbolizing the general ignorance and incompetence of the villains of the piece. The 'good news/bad news' routine cleverly reinforces our sense that the 'goodies' are really in con-trol and will win through, in spite of current incapacitation (see Figure 4.13).

The supposedly imminent destruction of the spaceship is shelved tem-porarily while Adrian pursues some humorous possibilities which he sud-denly sees for creating a pun on the literal and metaphorical uses of 'tied

```
"Quick! She's going to blow!"
"She's going down!"
"Turn the pressure up two kilowatts!"
"Turn the gas pipe down two litres!"
"Get the fire extinguishers!"
"We're going to crash!"
```

Figure 4.12

```
"OK. Do you want the bad news or the good news first?"
"Well, I'll tell you the bad news first and the good news last. It's
about to blow to bits. The good news is that we can fly it."
```

Figure 4.13

up'. Indeed, on re-reading, Adrian was most amused by his idea that the person who was supposed to be untying the captives so that they could fly the ship and save it was too 'tied up' in his work to do so, claiming that this was the 'best bit' (see Figure 4.14).

Many interesting possibilities were envisaged that never in the end became incorporated into text. For example, Adrian would discuss the meanings of words which he liked the sound of and would like to use (quadrilateral, hypothermia, curriculum) but whose meanings he did not really understand; or he would be wondering about whether to use a routine borrowed from *The Three Stooges* or an idea borrowed from *Dr. Who* which he thought might be boring or might be funny but he was not sure which. On another, he would be considering the possibilities of using swearing without causing offence ('How about hell – is that a swear word?') – exploring the real meanings of swear words and making up his own on realizing that most of them have religious connections ('I'm a Christian myself').

That Adrian sustained interest in this story over such a prolonged period struck me as quite remarkable, and a reflection of the seriousness of his commitment to the project he had devised for himself. It was as if, once the connection was made between his out-of-school knowledge and his in-school writing, his work in school suddenly gained an authority that had previously been absent, and a confidence to pursue his own project in spite of objections. Adrian's sense of his talent as a writer was confirmed by the experience with Kieran, releasing new energy as well as new resources to be channelled into his writing.

These developments were made possible by the opportunity provided by the workshop for Adrian to set his own purposes and pursue his own interests in his writing. The use of the class as an audience and source of support for one another's writing worked for Adrian not only as a spur but also as a resource, particularly in the later stages, as he used a sense of his audience's needs to work at telling a story to his own satisfaction through dia-

Figure 4.14

logue. He loved the fact that children had the right not to share their work with other children while it was being written, if they preferred, so that it could be a surprise when it was finished. The secrecy added to the pleasure of suspense, which, Adrian claimed, 'helps you with your writing'. Moreover, sharing his writing with others provided a way, I have suggested, of building bridges with other children through his writing that he might have found difficult to establish by other means. Including the other children as key characters in his story, with himself as the leader, and everyone working together for the same cause, helped to forge bonds that might otherwise have been beyond his reach.

It seemed to me, then, that Adrian's response to the opportunities of the writing workshop approach followed much more closely than Annette's the pattern anticipated by Graves' research. Freedom of topic choice played a central and crucial role in harnessing Adrian's commitment to writing. His writing intentions generated the problems to solve that challenged his existing resources and, at the same time, the impetus to persist in his efforts to write his ideas down, in spite of the extreme limitations of his existing secretarial skills. The collaborative learning environment provided an ever-present audience upon whom to try out ideas and from whom to receive feedback about the success of his writing in engaging and entertaining others.

However, the study helped me to appreciate that the task of building bridges between a child's out-of-school knowledge and experience and their experience in school may be more complicated than I had imagined. Indeed, my initially negative response to the influence of television prompts me to think that we may be more selective than we care to admit about what kinds of out-of-school experience we do, and do not, value. Or perhaps the lesson to be learnt is that, however 'examined' our cultural assumptions, the messages we intend to convey to children may not be the messages that they pick up, particularly if prior experience has led them to believe that much of what they know arising from their out-of-school experience is irrelevant or even wrong in the context of school.

Offering a child the opportunity to work collaboratively with an adult also poses a significant dilemma. On the one hand, scribing Adrian's work for him allowed him the satisfaction of achieving his purposes for writing and the opportunity to demonstrate (and so enable us to appreciate) the full extent of his compositional knowledge and skill. On the other hand, it removed the vital incentive that the workshop had created (by engaging his commitment) for him to work at developing his secretarial skills in purposeful language contexts. Whilst my collaboration with Adrian may have helped to seal the re-engagement of his commitment to the task of learning to write, it may also have diverted his energies away from developing the necessary tools through which to transcribe his vast reservoir of ideas for entertaining others into writing. The significance of the discrepancy between his ability to transcribe and ability to compose, and its implications for teaching will be examined in the final part of the chapter.

THE EYE OF THE BEHOLDER?

> One needs to be very sure indeed, in our view, before deciding that a child is not dyslexic.
>
> (Miles and Miles, 1983, p. 86)

One of my reasons for choosing Adrian as a focus for detailed study had been because of the huge discrepancy between his compositional knowledge and technical skill noted in my early encounters with his writing. I wanted to use my growing knowledge of his writing to help me revisit the debate surrounding dyslexia with a reasonably open mind. My concern was to ensure that, if we put the main emphasis on general curriculum development as a way of offering support, we should not overlook *other* vital sources of insight into children's learning needs, particularly if these applied only to a minority. For if Adrian's limited mastery of secretarial skills did signal some sort of underlying problem or disorder which had implications for teaching, then he would be disadvantaged as long as those particular needs were not recognized and provided for, whatever positive developments were achieved in other aspects of his writing.

I became somewhat distracted from these intentions during the course of the study because of the enormous challenges that I found myself facing in trying to develop the resources needed to describe Adrian's compositional abilities, and consider how the development of these was bound up with the specific features of the writing workshop. Adrian drew my attention to other limits of my understanding that I had not expected to spend time thinking about, and so limited the extent to which I was able to pursue these particular questions.

Consequently, my study of Adrian's secretarial skills and their possible links with dyslexia concentrates almost exclusively on spelling. There is clearly much more to pursue with respect to the significance of his limited development in handwriting but, for the reasons noted, it turned out to be more than could be tackled within the scope of one study. As a researcher without teaching responsibility for these children, I could allow myself the luxury of making a choice about where to focus my attention, and this is not intended to imply that concerns about handwriting are less significant than the issues I chose to pursue. Adrian was receiving help with his handwriting, as part of a systematic programme of handwriting teaching and practice built into the overall curriculum, and in addition to the writing undertaken for the writing workshop. The impact of this work was perhaps too recent, however, to show up in his spontaneous letter formation during draft-writing, when his mind was taken up with complex compositional ideas and the strenuous mental effort required for spelling.

My more limited aim, then, was to explore whether there appeared to be grounds for pursuing the possibility of dyslexia as a factor in Adrian's spelling. If so, what were the implications for the learning opportunities that needed to be provided, and could these be readily incorporated into the writing workshop? Using the literature on dyslexia to support this task was problematic, I found, because the books I consulted (Miles and Miles, 1983; Snowling, 1987; Pumfrey and Reason, 1992) made inferences, in attempting to describe the condition of dyslexia, that I was not comfortable with. What did seem potentially usable, for the purposes of qualitative analysis, was the idea of looking out for bizarre or unusual spellings that might be a sign of dyslexia. In my study of Adrian's spelling, I therefore kept a watch for such spellings as I attempted to build up an overall picture of what Adrian already knew, and how he was applying that knowledge to help him to tackle unfamiliar words. I had kept records of all Adrian's unaided attempts at words, alongside the completed texts. However, amongst all the examples, I found only one which struck me as in any way unusual, or rather where what Adrian produced seemed to me to be other than an expression of highly intelligent problem-solving. The main characteristics of his spelling that I identified were as follows.

Firstly, I was struck by how few known words Adrian seemed to draw ready-made in standard form from his memory store. This made spelling into a highly laborious and mentally taxing process because he was having to generate possible grapheme correspondences for every sound in every word, as he articulated them to himself in his mind, and then select from these a combination that made sense as nearly as he could tell. He actually did this very successfully. Because he was not used to being given words by the teacher or simply remembering them visually, he had become quite adept at holding a word stable in his mind, breaking it down into phonemes, and attempting to find letters to correspond to the sounds. His rendering of 'afared' for 'afraid' is a good example. If we imagine a child saying the word slowly, trying to break it down into segments (and guessing three rather than two syllables a-fa-red), we can see the logic of Adrian's version, even if the ending seems a poor rendering of -aid. Suggesting 'ed' as a word ending is, after all, a sensible guess (perhaps, even, as in 'frayed'?).

Even more striking, perhaps, was that in spite of the time this process took, Adrian was never discouraged from trying unknown words and indeed seemed genuinely interested in discovering more about how words worked. Because unusual words interested him and he prided himself in including in his writing words that other children did not use, he would blithely go ahead and attempt words that many children (in my experience) would assume they simply could not write ('essmt' for 'exterminate', 'wrouasem' for 'awesome', 'mordr' for 'murderer'). Maybe Adrian assumed that this was what spelling entailed, that it was what everyone did when spelling (except that some people can do it faster than others). I noticed that he continued to work out letter by letter even familiar, two and three letter words which he must have seen and written many times before. It seemed that somehow he had not learnt to co-ordinate his knowledge of sound – symbol relationships with the use of a visual memory store.

Far from finding his spelling bizarre or unusual, this part of the study forced me to completely revise my assessment of his secretarial skills, which I had previously been disposed to couch in very deficit-laden terms. What I had previously assumed to be 'considerable difficulty' with spelling even the most common words proved, on closer inspection, to represent a very considerable intellectual accomplishment. Far from being in the early stages of learning to spell, as his struggle with two and three letter words seemed to suggest, in fact his spelling showed signs, even in the early part of the study, that he was already moving into what Temple, Nathan and Burris, (1982) describe as the 'transitional' stage. This refers to the point when children can be seen beginning to extrapolate and apply rules of the spelling system to their invented spelling, rather than looking for straight phonemic correspondences. Adrian was doing something vastly more complex and intellectually sophisticated than learning 'correct' spelling. Looking at his invented spelling, we can see him working out spellings using the hypotheses he had already formed about how the spelling system worked. Indeed, he had already made considerable progress in discerning its rules and patterns.

For example, early on in the study, when Adrian (over an extended period of effort) produced 'Britten' for 'Britain', he was demonstrating an awareness of the marking rules governing the doubling of consonants, and developing hypotheses relating to the application of these. Thus, given the sequence of letters with which Adrian chose to spell 'Britain', it was appropriate to double the 't' in order to maintain the short vowel sound of the 'i', when the 't' was followed by an 'e'. When he wrote 'essmt' (for exterminate), Adrian made a choice to double the 's' to reflect the soft sound (as in 'essential', 'dress') rather, say, than the hard sound of 's' like a 'z' (as in 'armies'). When he wrote 'Earmy' for 'army', he may have been making a connection with 'Earth' which he had just worked out (hoping that the same unlikely sequence of letters might work again!); however, the 'y' at the end shows that his understanding of spelling has moved beyond an attempt to simply to match phonemes with a corresponding letter (in which case he would probably have chosen 'e').

Other attempts to apply rules, can be seen in Adrian's rendering of 'sir' as 'sore', indicating that he is aware that some words have a silent 'e' at the end and is working out the situations where this rule applies (also 'or' as in 'word'?); in 'msheing' for machine, we see Adrian trying to locate a use for 'ing', perhaps replacing the notion of a silent 'e' here with a silent 'g'; when he writes 'coun' for 'can', he experiments with the possibility of two vowels coming in sequence, moreover, he chooses not just *any* two vowels, but those in 'could' which, indeed, correspond much more closely to the sound made by 'can' in the context of use. (In 'I can look after myself, you know', the way 'can' would be spoken sounds far more like the 'ou' in 'could' than the 'a' in 'cat' or 'can').

Adrian seemed to be working on clarifying the function of vowels, and particularly the use of double vowels within words. As well as 'coun' and 'wrouasem', he also explored 'louts' for 'lots' and 'poel' for people. He had not worked out yet the need for double 'e' in 'sem' (seem) although, as we have seen, he had discovered the possibility of a silent 'e' at the end of words and was exploring its application.

As I examined his spelling more closely, then, I began to see his inventions not as the efforts of someone who is having difficulties with mastering spelling but rather as astonishing achievements of someone who is successfully negotiating his way through a highly complex process of hypothesis testing and generalization in relation to the workings of the writing system. He always knew enough to have a go, before asking for help, for example producing unaided 'inc-od' for 'include', leaving the space to indicate that he knew a letter was missing.

The one example that stood out was Adrian's rendering of 'fighting' as 'femingt'. My impression was that here, exceptionally, Adrian had failed to hold the word stable and identify the phonemes with any (to my mind) recognizable logic. The 'f' and 't' indicate that he had identified the key consonants although I do not see why the 't' is placed at the end. Clearly there was a flash of inspiration as he discovered an application for 'ing', but I simply cannot make sense of the 'em' at the beginning. Perhaps, in the context in which this word was produced (the title for his piece 'Dr Who and the Awesome Fighting Machine') the sheer effort of producing these three complex unphonetic spellings in a row was simply too much to maintain quite such a highly rigorous standard of analysis.

To see if perhaps I was missing something, I referred back to some of the examples of children's spelling in the literature previously consulted on dyslexia. I was taken aback to discover, amongst the examples discussed, that what seemed to me to be intelligent renderings of word spellings (similar to Adrian's) were interpreted as evidence of 'confusion' on the part of the child. A child's rendering of 'substance', for example, as 'sepedns' was seen as reflecting a confusion on the child's part between 'b' and 'p'. But unless one *already* knows that the words is spelt with a 'b' not a 'p' then the vocalization of the sound in 'substance' in fact sounds far more like a 'p' than a 'b'. Try saying 'sup' and then 'substance' and see if you could tell the difference if you did not already know what the spelling was. It could be, then, that my intention to seek something 'unusual' intrinsic to the data was misconceived: that meaning is in the eye of the beholder, and the same data will be interpreted as a 'problem' or 'intelligent hypothesizing' by observers with different orientations.

Thus my study of Adrian's spelling did not, after all, provide me with the opportunity I was hoping for to challenge and develop my thinking about dyslexia. My analysis suggested that there was every sign that Adrian was establishing a sound basis of knowledge, by the criteria informing current thinking on processes of literacy development (Temple, Nathan and Burris, 1982), and that he had the resources from which to continue to generate appropriate insights into the spelling system through his own experience of writing. 'Making progress in spelling is like making progress in playing chess. Both require enthusiastic commitment not only of the memory, but of the intellect as well' (Temple, Nathan and Burris, 1982, p. 120).

Over the period of the study, Adrian gained considerably in the greater confidence and speed with which he was able to tackle his writing. Whereas, in the early days, to write one word would take several minutes of intense effort, by the latter part of the year, Adrian was able to produce a piece in which he was giving the same degree of careful thought to the process of composition in a fraction of the time. He had become much more practised in applying his knowledge of spelling patterns to unfamiliar words, with the result that he was able to transcribe his ideas in far less time and with less labour than previously. Thus, the piece shown in Figure 4.15 (though admittedly difficult to decipher) was written in less than ten minutes.

It was by no means the case that children were left to 'discover' spelling for themselves. Spelling was taught in the context of children's own writing, and children were always asked to try a word out, rather than being given a spelling, in order to encourage them to develop their own hypotheses and allow the teacher access to these in their invented spelling. Nevertheless, from the specific characteristics of Adrian's spelling identified earlier, it does seem that he was complicating the task for himself in various ways.

''OK, what does it do?''
''It has great lifting powers''
''It doesn't seem to be working''
''What do you call this?''
''This is all very well, but where's Afia?''
''I can look after myself, you know.''
''Afia, where were you?''

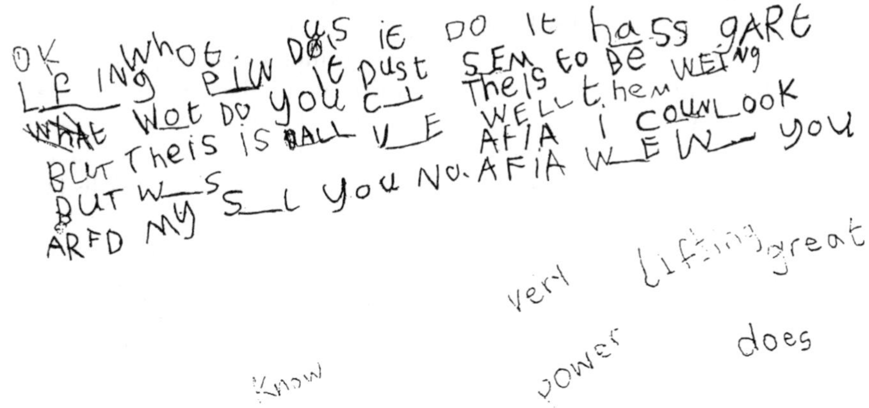

Figure 4.15

Whereas most children would adjust the content of what they wrote to what they knew, more or less, they could write with reasonable ease, Adrian would pursue whatever entertaining ideas occurred to him, irrespective of whether he could write the word or not. Hence he gave himself fewer opportunities to consolidate a body of known material which he could draw on to speed up the process of writing, and also use as a resource against which to check out developing hypotheses, to speed up understanding of rules. The spelling book which he had started was thus not a lot of help in the long run, because the words he needed more often than not were not contained in it. Such a book might be useful, however, in helping him more systematically and rigorously to learn spellings of common words, perhaps making the task less laborious for himself by making more appropriate use of visual memory. Admittedly, since he was an inexperienced reader, reading was maybe not a very powerful source of visual information; but almost certainly his learning would be facilitated by complementing his existing strategies with more emphasis on visual memory.

IMPLICATIONS FOR PRACTICE

Whilst I would argue that there is every reason to feel optimistic about Adrian's spelling development, I would nevertheless agree that there is also reason to be concerned about the discrepancy between his overall knowledge and skill with regard to the writing process and his secretarial skills. To the extent that independent writing is the medium for assessment, there is clearly a risk that Adrian's abilities will be underestimated, not just in rela-tion to the writing process but across all areas of the curriculum. We have seen how Adrian's opportunities to display, use and develop his abilities through the medium of the written word were continually constrained by the sheer effort involved in producing a few lines of writing. Thus his level of functioning across the curriculum could be dictated and/or defined by the stage of development of his handwriting and spelling.

Recognition of this risk to Adrian might prompt a more general re-exam-ination of the range of opportunities provided within the curriculum to learn and demonstrate learning other than through the medium of the written word. In the area of assessment of writing, it underscores the importance of maintaining separate assessment of compositional and secretarial skills (abol-ished in the new Orders for the National Curriculum).

On the other hand, if we introduce methods which by-pass dependence upon writing, we then may deprive the child of equally important opportu-nities to use and develop writing purposefully as part of normal learning activities. Alongside the responsibility to ensure that children with limited secretarial skills are not unnecessarily disadvantaged by the traditional cur-ricular emphasis upon writing, there is a second kind of responsibility to review and re-examine the adequacy of opportunities currently provided for children to enhance and develop their skills. If we do not conceptualize our task, therefore, in terms of both these responsibilities, then the consequent lack of opportunity will directly contribute to the continued disadvantage of the child.

Moreover, the study has helped to uncover other ways in which the lim-itations of our thinking may operate to the disadvantage of children. Studying Adrian's response has raised in my awareness the possibility that we might fail to appreciate the significance of a child's development either because we lack the concepts and resources to identify and describe what is significant about it, or because we are trying to impose on the pattern of the child's development a preconceived idea of what learning is or ought to look like that does not fit that demonstrated by the child.

It was only because I found that I could not account for Adrian's progress in the manner I had done for Annette that I was prompted to question the cumulative, linear growth model that underpinned the way that I had set about identifying progress in Annette's case.

> 'And chaos theory teaches us' Malcolm said, 'that straight linearity, which we have come to take for granted in everything from physics to fiction, simply does not exist. Linearity is an artificial way of viewing the world. Real life isn't a series of interconnected events occurring one after another like beads strung on a necklace. Life is actually a series of encounters in which one event may change those that follow in a wholly unpredictable . . . way.'
>
> (Crichton, 1991, p. 172)

If we apply a linear model to Adrian's writing and find no clear evidence of development, do we stop to consider that it might be the model that is lack-ing rather than features of Adrian's writing development? Thinking about the development of my own compositional knowledge since I began to write with a genuine intent to communicate a message to an audience (which is what Adrian was already doing), I have to acknowledge that the learning process is indeed akin to the one that Adrian arranged for himself within the range of possibilities provided by the workshop approach. It is more a matter of *broadening experience* than of logical progression in a prescribed direction. The direction is dictated by the nature of the task, and the nature of the task by the purposes of the individual. Growth occurs through experience of successfully tackling the exigencies of a particular task.

I am reminded of the distinction made by Goldstein and Noss (1990) between a model of learning as the ascent of a mountain and a model of learning as a visit to an exhibition. In the first case, there is only one way to go, and the aim is to get to the top. In the second case, there is indeed a logic to the arrangement of the exhibits but no inexorable order. Visitors can stop as long as they like at particular exhibits and return to them again and again, with new purposes and fresh interest. This, it seems to me, is what Adrian was doing over the period that I studied him: visiting different kinds of writing in order to experiment with the genre, depending upon his particular interests at the time and also, perhaps, (as was noted briefly) upon his emotional needs. Each of these different kinds of writing generated their own exigencies, according to the particular purposes that he had in mind.

We can tell he was learning, not because we can set (very different) pieces of work alongside one another and ascertain the difference between them, but because his intentions for writing were generating problems that he was successfully tackling. By definition, problems encountered in writing reflect the limits of existing knowledge, otherwise they would be tackled successfully without ever emerging as problems to be solved. In this way, we define development and growth intrinsically, through the range of tasks undertaken and the nature of problems addressed.

Admittedly, this is a far cry from prescribed criteria and levels of attainment against which individual children's abilities are to be statutorily assessed, and against which no doubt 'learning difficulties' will be defined. Indeed, Adrian's story provides the resources for a powerful case to be made about the injustices that may follow for some children from the new statutory procedures for assessment, particularly paper and pencil tests, and their potential for contributing, contrary to popular belief and political intention, to a *lowering* of standards in schools.

5

The Dynamics of Learning and Teaching

These two studies of children's writing development were carried out in circumstances very different from those of a busy teacher, so they are clearly not intended to replicate practice. What they provide is an opportunity to see inside a process of learning – my own, bound up with that of each child – and so to examine anew the *complexities* involved for teachers, in the ordinary circumstances of practice, in attempting to make sense of and respond sensitively and appropriately to every child. They provide the means to review and appreciate afresh the *possibilities* bound up with the complexities of teaching, and upon which the approach proposed in this book is based.

As the immediate and principal source of these ideas, the stories provide the concrete detail that will enable me to illustrate, develop and give further grounding to the theory and practice of innovative thinking as explained in the initial chapters. The challenge, in particular, for the remainder of the book, is to make a convincing case that pursuing concerns about children's learning by studying the dynamics of classroom experience is not only possible and fruitful in the context of research, but is also feasible within the constraints of everyday teaching.

The research did eventually enable me to resolve some of my original concerns about support work and reach a new understanding of the support teacher's role. For a time, though, these issues were set to one side, while I worked through new questions raised by the research and began to re-think my earlier perception of the wider task. I had started out with a seemingly unshakeable conviction that the most just and constructive way to provide support for children experiencing difficulties was (principally) through general developments in the curriculum intended to benefit all children. Through the research, however, I discovered that even this apparently broad focus for development work was far too narrowly conceived. My studies of these two children's learning drew attention to the need for a much more sophisticated understanding of the scope that exists within mainstream education for enhancing children's learning, and highlighted the central place of teachers' thinking in its discovery and realization. In this chapter, I draw on the two stories to help explain the two key insights which brought about this shift of emphasis, and show how they contributed to the evolution of an approach based on innovative thinking.

THE UNPREDICTABILITY OF CHILDREN'S LEARNING

The research made me realize, firstly, how vulnerable even our best worked-out theories are to the complexities of classroom experience. However carefully we have formulated ideas about what might be done to make the curriculum more supportive, it is impossible to legislate in advance for what will *happen* when these ideas become part of the complex dynamics at work in a particular situation. Many *other* aspects of the situation, which have a bearing on children's learning, come into play in unexpected and unpredictable ways and turn our good intentions into something which is always different from what we expected and sometimes completely at odds with what we intended.

In Adrian's case, the outcome seemed to endorse my prior expectation about conditions for writing development that would be supportive of children's learning. Yet the study still led into unanticipated areas. The analysis required in order to appreciate how Adrian was making use of the opportunities provided by the writing workshop was far more complex than anything that had been in my mind when I had identified its specific features as likely to be supportive of children's learning. His response depended upon a unique constellation of circumstances, associated with his writing abilities, his recent arrival in the class, his status as a newcomer in the peer group, his perception of himself as a writer, a teacher's timely intervention, and so on. The particular features of the writing workshop were supportive in a unique and individual-specific way: they allowed him to use his talent for writing to solve the problem of how to build relationships and make friends, and to use his desire to entertain the audience-who-would-be-his-friends to fire his commitment and provide the cutting edge for his thinking in developing his writing.

In Annette's case, the outcome was far more unexpected and ambiguous. The strategy which she invented to cope with the threats posed by freedom of topic choice and a collaborative learning environment certainly did play a critical role, according to my analysis, in setting her back on the path to independent learning. But the dynamics which brought this outcome about were not at all consistent with the rationale that had led me to believe that these specific features of the writing workshop would be supportive of children's learning. My analysis suggested, too, that there were aspects of the repertoire-writing strategy which could be a hindrance to subsequent learning unless some specific initiative was taken by Annette or her teachers to develop the understandings and skills that she was seeking to compensate for.

Annette provided a salutory lesson about the gap between our *intentions* and what actually *happens* when our good theories about how to develop a curriculum supportive of children's learning become absorbed into the complex dynamics of the classroom and filtered through children's own systems of meaning. She made me realize that *any* strategies we introduce with a view to developing a more supportive curriculum will be vulnerable to the same fate, once they take on a life of their own and come into interaction with children's agendas and with all the other influences in the situation that have a bearing on children's learning

To acknowledge this unpredictability, as an inevitable feature of the dynamics of learning and teaching, is not to imply that there is no point in attempting to pursue general ideas for making the curriculum more supportive for all children. It is simply to acknowledge that, however good the rationale behind these ideas, there will always be more thinking to do at the point of children's engagement with curriculum experience. We cannot know in advance how the dynamics will work themselves through in the case of each child. Therefore much depends upon the teacher's ability to think on the spot – or afterwards – when we have access to the evidence which will allow us to see what further intervention might be possible or necessary to help smooth the child's path to learning. At that point, the analysis necessarily has to be *individualized*: examining the dynamics shaping the child's learning, and seeking out new insights that can be used to guide our response.

The implication, then, is that the thinking which teachers do moment by moment in their classrooms – and retrospectively in reviewing the learning of individual children – is at least as important to the task of opening up new possibilities for enhancing children's learning as the best laid plans that we formulate in advance of teaching. My studies of Annette and Adrian highlighted the vital contribution that such individually-focused analysis can make to the overall process of opening up new possibilities for enhancing children's learning within mainstream education. They showed that insights deriving from individualized analysis do more than suggest new ideas for supporting individual children's development. They open up all sorts of other, quite unexpected areas, and point in many new directions for the development of practice that we might not otherwise have been prompted to think about.

For example, Annette's repertoire-writing strategy alerted me to the role that a repertoire plays in everybody's writing. It set me thinking about how children acquire their individual repertoires, and what teaching and learning practices might most effectively support their extension and development. Annette made me think afresh about how children acquire their concepts of writing, and how the way that we organize the teaching and learning of writing influences, for better or worse, the development of that concept. She raised anew the question of how children learn to put together extended texts of different kinds, and whether specific teaching is needed. She reminded me of the need to make explicit to children the connection between reading and writing, and to review how effectively existing practice supports children in making that connection.

Adrian helped me to appreciate in a new way how television literacy could strengthen and inform the development of print-based literacy in school, as well as how this connection helped to make sense of the unique qualities and characteristics of his activities and development in writing over the period of the study. He changed my perception of the educative potential of television-watching, and set me wondering about the extent to which other children might have similar untapped resources of television literacy. How might they be encouraged to use and build on in the development of print-based literacy? How might the television literacy which all children have developed before starting school, be harnessed and built on from the earliest days in school? What difference would it make to children's acquisition of literacy if we were to build on their knowledge of narrative acquired through television as well as that acquired by listening to stories read aloud? How would we do this?

As well as providing new insights into the teaching and learning of writing, the two accounts also served to prompt some new thinking about teaching, learning and assessment generally. Annette helped me to appreciate in a new way that in order to make judgements about a child's progress and help towards the next steps in learning, we need to take account of the child's purposes and agenda for learning, and try to see what might count as progress from the child's point of view. Adrian caused me to think about alternative models of learning and how the model we instinctively use affects the conclusions that we reach. As well as subtly changing the way we value and respond to the learning of particular individuals, such insights affect our thinking in ways which influence and foster the development of our overall work with children.

To summarize, the research made me see that my faith in general curriculum development – as a more just and constructive alternative to additional support for individual children – was far less securely based that I had realized. The inherent unpredictability of children's learning demands a much more sophisticated understanding and response than was reflected in my earlier thinking. The active part children play in shaping classroom processes is part of what makes the teacher's task so complex. However, it is also what creates its inherent possibilities. In seeking to unravel and enhance our understanding of these complex dynamics shaping children's responses, we can be confident that new ideas will emerge which extend, enrich and challenge our thinking in a way that potentially benefits all children.

THE COMPLEXITIES OF CLASSROOM DECISION-MAKING

Growing realization of the limitations of my original focus upon general curriculum development was also fuelled by another set of concerns. These were related to the unexpected difficulties which I found myself experiencing in making sense of Annette's and Adrian's learning during the course of the research. In Annette's case, the main reason for my confusion was because there seemed to be so many interpretations that could be made of the same evidence, and every interpretation I came up with seemed to be open to question from another point of view. In Adrian's case, I was suddenly not sure how best to proceed, partly because I could see that I lacked important information that was needed and partly because I did not feel that I had adequate resources to carry out the proposed analysis.

Initially, I saw these as methodological problems needing to be resolved before I could reach conclusions about their development that would help to answer my research questions. Gradually, though, I began to see that they were drawing attention to a whole dimension of classroom experience that had not been included in my original perception of the task. This was the area of teachers' moment-by-moment thinking and decision-making with respect to individual children and the impact which this has upon children's subsequent learning. Examining this area in my attempts to resolve my own difficulties allowed me to appreciate a new set of possibilities for enhancing learning, far less time-consuming and grandiose in scale than the possibilities that I had been envisaging, yet just as crucial and important from the perspective of individual children.

At first, I assumed that the difficulties that I was experiencing probably stemmed from not having a direct teaching responsibility towards Annette and Adrian. This meant that I had no opportunity to test out my developing understandings through dialogue with the child and through action as teachers usually do. So I could not use the feedback provided by children's words and behaviour to judge the adequacy of my understandings and adjust them accordingly. My research role also meant that I had a far more limited knowledge of the children and the situation than I would have been working from had I been their teacher. A teacher interprets present activity not simply in terms of everything else that is going on in the classroom at that moment, but what has been going on previously and her entire prior knowledge of the child and of other children in the group. My intermittent presence meant that I only had access to a very limited part of that information.

As I was working out how these difficulties might best be resolved for the purposes of the research, however, I found myself drawing parallels with teachers' moment-by-moment thinking and decision-making in practice. I started thinking about the consequences, for children's learning, of how such difficulties are resolved – or perhaps glossed over – in the course of everyday teaching. Although the circumstances of the research were clearly different, it struck me that the task of making sense of children's learning in practice does indeed share many of the same constraints and difficulties. The difference is that, in a busy classroom, we have less time to become aware of them and worry about their implications for children's learning. In practice, the information base we are working from is always partial and incomplete. The knowledge, experience and expertise which we bring to the task is always, inevitably, limited. Since we are constantly under pressure to move to judgement and action, much of the time we also have to work from the understandings and possibilities which immediately spring to mind, because there is too little time to deliberate alternative possibilities.

Limitations of immediate interpretations

I realized how much unexamined thinking there inevitably is bound up in our moment-by-moment interpretations and how much is *missed*, in the course of ordinary teaching, if this thinking is left unexamined. It was salutory to see all the possibilities that could be brought to mind, given time to reflect, beyond my initial spontaneous interpretations. It was even more salutory to see how earlier interpretations quite often changed into a quite different perception of the child's learning, as a result of new information that became available subsequently or new understandings which shed new light on earlier meanings.

In Annette's story, for instance, it was only with the benefit of hindsight that I was able to see the significance of some of the things that happened and had puzzled me in the early part of the study. It was only once the pattern of her development suggested to me the idea of repertoire-writing that I was able to see in a quite different light (what I had perceived as) unexpectedly dull writing which she produced immediately after abandoning drawing. Similarly, my view of the repetitive routines which she continually rehearsed in her writing changed, during the course of the research, to an admiration of the ingenuity which lay behind this strategy and a new appreciation of the contribution that repetition specifically had played in restoring her confidence and setting her back on the path to independent learning.

In Adrian's case, my taken-for-granted assumption that he had difficulties with spelling, was subsequently revised as I studied the thinking reflected in his invented spelling and began to appreciate what he was doing as highly intelligent, problem-solving activity. The disagreement between Adrian and his teachers over the limitations of his dialogue-writing also came to be seen later in a somewhat different light. At the time – much to Adrian's annoyance – we all thought that he was neglecting important aspects of narrative and needed to build these in around his dialogue, assuming that the problem lay in the limits of *Adrian's* understanding of how to embed dialogue within narrative. It was only much later that an alternative reading of that situation occurred to me, which suggested that what made us perceive Adrian's writing as problematic might have been a reflection of the limits of our understandings rather than his.

The experience underlined again and again how cautious we must be about the authority that we give to *any* interpretations of children's learning, and especially those which construct the meaning of the situation in terms of deficiencies of the *child's* understanding. Our interpretations are constructed through a process of meaning-making which is highly complex and uncertain. The understandings we reach depend upon the possibilities that we consider, which in turn depend upon the limited time, information and resources available to us. It is always possible, therefore, that retrospectively we will discover a new meaning which shows the child's activity in a quite different light. We may not be able to see that potential at this point, but we do need to acknowledge its existence in principle. We need to keep an open mind so that we are receptive to developments that would open up new possibilities. Every act of investing meaning simultaneously excludes alternative possibilities, and those alternatives may be lost from view permanently if we do not have time to go back and review our earlier thinking in the light of subsequent experience, or if it does not occur to us to question existing interpretations.

From thinking to action

The process of translating *thinking* into *action* also entails choosing between many alternative possibilities. Yet there are no clear-cut prescriptions to follow about the action to take in the light of particular understandings. How do we decide what to do, based on whatever judgement we have reached? How do these decisions affect the subsequent learning of individual children? How do we make a choice, when there is much controversy and disagreement about teaching approaches in a particular area?

This is the case at the moment, for example, with respect to the polarization of views over the teaching of reading (e.g. Turner, 1990). In Annette's story, exploring the practical implications of her seemingly limited understanding about how to construct extended text led into similarly disputed territory. On the one hand, there are persuasive arguments that children need explicit, structured teaching of the conventions of narrative and other written genres, and not to provide such explicit teaching would be to seriously disadvantage the child. On the other hand, others are highly critical of genre theory and argue with equal force that such teaching is more likely to inhibit than foster writing development. They would prefer other strategies, for example encouraging children to experiment with writing about topics of genuine personal significance, supported by reading which exposes them to a wide range of genres.

How do we decide, then, what is an appropriate strategy? How do we gain and develop the knowledge that informs our decision-making? What possibilities are ruled out or not considered in the process? And what are the consequences for children's learning? As the dilemmas surrounding my involvement as Adrian's scribe illustrate, strategies that are sound in themselves may nevertheless still have a limiting effect on the child's learning if they over-emphasize one kind of response at the expense of another. In the case of Adrian's limited secretarial skills, a balance needed to be established between strategies designed to *promote the development of* his secretarial skills and those designed to ensure that other learning was not *inhibited by* his limitations in this area. An imbalance in either direction could serve to impede his overall development.

The complexities of the teacher's task

Moreover, it is not just time and the pressure of numbers which prevents us from noticing and pursuing some of the possibilities available to us. It is also the sheer complexity of the teacher's task in attempting to penetrate the meaning of children's responses, establish when help is required and decide an appropriate response. My study of Annette, for instance, drew my attention to how we might unwittingly confuse, disorient or provoke resistance in a child if the strategy we adopt to support learning does not take account of possible differences between teachers' meanings and children's meanings and seek to understand what might count as the next step in the child's learning from the child's point of view. There was a moment when Annette refused a very carefully prepared and negotiated opportunity to receive feedback on her writing, when her teacher felt that she should now be beginning to move on to re-drafting her writing. Examining the reasons why she might have resisted this (even though she seemed quite keen on the idea at the time), it occurred to me that perhaps the task made no sense to Annette (except as another demand of school which she would seek to fulfil) because it did not fit with her current perception of what she was trying to do with her writing.

Annette's story serves to illustrate, too, circumstances that may militate against a need for help even coming to our attention. Children's own strategies for coping with the demands of classroom life may precisely be designed to obscure from us the nature of the help that is required. Annette's repertoire-writing strategy was designed to enable her to be successful in her own terms *without* the knowledge and skills that as yet eluded her. Its success in fostering her progress in other areas, coupled with our desire to celebrate that success, might therefore prevent us from noticing its more problematic aspects and the steps that needed to be taken to foster and promote further learning.

Through the experience of the research, then, I became more aware of all the possibilities for understanding and responding to children's learning which so quickly slip past, or pass unnoticed, under the constraints of ordinary practice. It made me think about the cumulative effect of teachers' moment-by-moment thinking and decision-making upon children's learning and development in the long term. What difference might it make to children's learning if we were to open up more systematically these processes of thinking and decision-making to examination? What difference would it make if we were able to recover and pursue some of these alternative possibilities?

A POSITIVE RATIONALE

These two strands of the research seemed to be pointing towards similar conclusions. My original argument had been that responding to concerns about children's learning through the provision of additional adult support tends to divert attention and resources away from wider opportunities for building more supportive conditions for learning into the overall curriculum. Now, as a result of the research, I was able to see the limitations of even this apparently broad perception of the task. It gave far too little consideration to the agency of individuals – both teachers and children – in the complex interactions which make up school experience and help to shape its outcomes for individual children.

As the analysis in this chapter shows, a far more sophisticated understanding is needed of the scope available to teachers for enhancing children's learning, and that teachers' thinking is the key to its discovery and realization. The dynamics of learning and teaching are so complex that any learning situation is rich in potential for yielding new insights and understandings that can be translated into new ideas for supporting and enhancing children's learning in practice. This is the fundamental principle upon which the approach proposed in this book is based.

The stories illustrate the kinds of insights that can be opened up through an analysis designed to explore more systematically our own thinking about children's learning and the meaning of their responses to school experience. They show that if teachers do use their thinking powers in this way – to the extent that this is feasible within the constraints of everyday practice – the insights achieved can serve a double purpose. They provide a source of new ideas and strategies for supporting the learning of the individual who has been the focus of the analysis – many of which can be implemented either on an individual basis or incorporated into the work of the whole class. They also extend, enrich and challenge our thinking about teaching and learning in a way that potentially benefits all children.

There are many constraints, apart from just time which, deter teachers from using their thinking powers in this way, in response to concerns about children's learning. Other prevailing ways of thinking about and making sense of children's learning – or failure to learn – undermine teachers' sense of their own power to make a difference to the outcomes of education. Determinist ideas about ability and educability continually present us with the possibility that limitations of existing attainment might be a reflection of ceilings of innate or acquired ability determined by factors largely beyond teachers' control. The language of learning difficulties and special needs creates the impression that there exists a distinct group of children whose capabilities and needs are different from those of the majority. They raise doubts in teachers' minds about the relevance of their own expertise and resources. Indeed, teachers question if they should, in the interests of children, keep searching for solutions themselves or refer the child on to someone with more time and training to offer appropriate support.

That is why I believe that we need to set aside once and for all the language of learning difficulties and special needs if we are to become able to exploit more fully the scope available to us for enhancing children's learning. The notion of learning difficulties imposes a ready-made meaning on a situation causing concern, which is already disconnected from thinking that produced it. It is ill-fitted to an approach which accepts from the outset that perceived 'difficulties' may turn out to be a reflection of the limits of our own current understanding, and where absence of overt difficulties – as in Annette's case – can equally well become an occasion for concern. We need to replace it with a language that recognizes that, whatever the initial perception of the situation that gives rise to concern, the perception itself will change as we probe the dynamics at work and reach out for new understandings. We need a language that does not assume that the insights opened up through this transformative process apply only to a given individual, even though the analysis itself, and the understandings it leads to, are highly individualized.

The search for alternative ways of thinking about and pursuing concerns about children's learning has been a priority for many educators working in the special needs field for a number of years now, as a result of dissatisfaction with the concept of special educational needs introduced by the Warnock

Report (DES, 1978). Successive attempts have been made to develop a new language and rationale for redirecting attention to possibilities within mainstream education. For example, the notion of 'mismatch' has been proposed as a means of encouraging a broader understanding of the factors contributing to 'learning difficulties'. 'Learning difficulties' are seen not purely as a consequence of specific characteristics of the child, but of the encounter between child and school experience. According to this view, then if a child has a difficulty, we can assume that some sort of mismatch exists, between the child and the learning opportunities provided, and focus our attention on making the necessary adjustments so that successful learning is once more possible.

It has also been widely argued that the distinction between 'ordinary' and 'special' needs should be abandoned. The intention of positive discrimination implied by the notion of 'special' label can itself have unintended negative effects on the child and on teachers, whose behaviour and expectations may subtly be changed once the label has been applied. Since all children are unique and have their own 'special' or rather 'individual' needs, it is argued that the task should be to develop schools' flexibility to accommodate and be responsive to individual needs and differences (Dyson, 1990).

Research in the field of school effectiveness and school improvement has also been influential (Ainscow, 1991; Dyson and Gains, 1993). The case is now increasingly put forward that, rather than constructing elaborate systems of support for individual children, we should concentrate on making teaching more effective for all children (Ainscow and Tweddle, 1988). The task of responding to children experiencing difficulties can play a key part in improving education generally, if we interpret 'difficulties' as indicators of possibilities for reform of features of the curriculum and organization of schools. The 'special needs' task can be reconceptualized as a process of school improvement.

All these developments have had a common underlying thrust: to draw attention to previously unexplored possibilities for development within mainstream education and make these central rather than peripheral to the task of pursuing concerns about children's learning. All have been, or are, intended to carry a positive and empowering message for teachers. Nevertheless the message that is heard by teachers is often an implied criticism of existing practice.

The research helped me recognize in this newly emerging language of *unexplored possibilities* the potential for developing a genuinely positive rationale for redirecting attention to mainstream education which carries no implicit negative messages for teachers. As the analysis of this chapter has shown, any learning situation will be rich in possibilities just by virtue of the complexity of the teacher's task, the pressures under which teachers work and the inherent unpredictability of children's learning. These possibilities will be there, however expert and experienced the teacher, and however effective the school. Finding them depends upon teachers engaging in the kinds of analysis that lead on to new understanding. It is an expression of expertise, not an admission of the shortcomings of existing practice. Indeed, the more knowledge, experience and expertise teachers can bring to the task of understanding and responding to concerns about children's learning, the greater will be their ability to generate new ideas and possibilities to guide their work with children.

It occurred to me that perhaps some of the limitations and frustrations relating to support work that had prompted the research in the first place were due to the fact that we had not yet succeeded in developing a genuinely positive rationale for focusing on possibilities within mainstream education. We had changed explanations, theories and, in some cases, the terms that we were using, but we had not entirely escaped from the underlying *ways of thinking* associated with the language of 'learning difficulties'. We were still formulating the task in terms of a *deficiency* or limitation of some kind (if not in the child, then in the curriculum, in the system) which could be remedied, improved or circumvented in order to foster more successful learning.

The analysis in this chapter has proposed a qualitatively different account of why we should respond to concerns about children's learning by pursuing possibilities within mainstream education. Rooted in the positive language of *possibility* rather than pathology or deficiency, this rationale is founded upon an appreciation of the complexities of the educator's task and recognizes the subtlety of the thinking required to find and exploit previously unexplored possibilities. It may therefore have the potential to engage the energy and commitment of teachers more whole-heartedly than we have succeeded in doing up until now. Only if mainstream teachers do feel inspired to use their thinking powers more fully for this purpose will we begin to tap the vast reservoir of mainstream knowledge, understanding and expertise which for too long has been under-used.

6

Establishing a Sound Basis for Action

In the previous chapter, I explained how I arrived at the principle upon which the approach proposed in this book is based. I used the detail of the two stories to explain the basis for belief that any learning situation will be rich in potential for yielding new insights and understandings which can be translated into new ideas for supporting and enhancing children's learning in practice. If we accept this principle, we can use the knowledge and understanding upon which it is founded to structure, support and guide our responses to concerns about children's learning. We will automatically turn first to a search for as yet unexplored possibilities within our own thinking and teaching, and take more conscious and deliberate steps to seek them out. As the two stories show, a close study of individual children's learning does not necessarily lead to a narrow, purely individualized range of responses. A searching analysis of the highly specific meanings of one child's responses to school learning can yield ideas and possibilities for development of practice which extend well beyond the immediate situation and child upon whom attention is focused. It can provide a unique source of insight into significant pedagogical questions and possibilities worth pursuing to the potential benefit of all children.

However, the successful development of an approach based on this principle requires more than just positive commitment on the part of teachers to investing time in doing the kinds of thinking that help generate new understandings and possibilities for practice. As the difficulties encountered in making sense of Annette's and Adrian's learning illustrate, taking time to explore alternative possibilities may have the effect of increasing uncertainty about the meanings of children's classroom responses and what might best be done to support and enhance their learning. Given the complexities of the interpretive task, we need to establish means of assuring ourselves that new ideas emerging from such an analysis are indeed soundly based. New ideas are not automatically worth pursuing just by virtue of the fact that they are new. We have a responsibiity to ensure that any conclusions we reach are sufficiently sound to have confidence in using hypotheses derived from them to guide our work with children whose learning gives cause for concern.

In this chapter, I explain how the research enabled me to identify the kinds of thinking that allow us to have confidence in the sound basis of new ideas, and show that these are *also* the kinds of thinking that facilitate the trans-formation of existing concerns into new understandings. I examine the nature of the knowledge base upon which this thinking depends and consider the vital part that the ideas and perspectives of others can play in strengthening our thinking powers, and extending the range of possibilities that we are able to generate ourselves.

A MULTIPLICITY OF MEANINGS?

The question of how we can ensure that our thinking is sound arose for me in the course of the research because – even once the two accounts were written – I was still conscious that many of the uncertainties were by no means definitively resolved. I had no doubt that other accounts of the chil-dren's learning that could equally well have been made by *others* (with equal knowledge of the situation), or even by *myself* had I carried out the study some years earlier or later, or if I had made choices differently, on this occa-sion, during the course of the analysis. How, then, was I to have confidence in, and claim legitimacy for, these two particular accounts, knowing that oth-ers could have been written? How could I acknowledge the possibility of others, without thereby invalidating my own?

The accounts would certainly have been different, for example, if I had gone ahead with the idea of perhaps drawing on the work of Armstrong (1980) and/or Steedman (1982) to help me in my analysis of the content of the children's writing. Both were authors whose work, and thinking, I had greatly admired on first reading, and found myself returning to frequently over a number of years. Armstrong's approach is to carry out a careful tex-tual analysis of the way that the child has used language to construct mean-ing, giving this the same serious attention and critical examination as would more typically be given, by literary critics, to works of literature (Armstrong, 1980, 1990). Steedman presents a fascinating *cultural* reading of a story writ-ten collaboratively by four girls in her class, showing how the themes which it develops pick up on and explore the writers' experience as girls growing up to be women under particular social and historical circumstances.

In the end I decided against trying to borrow from the approaches of either or both of these writers, largely because I felt insecure using others' frameworks. I preferred to rely more directly on my own more familiar ways of making sense of children's learning, drawing on the ideas of others as these occurred naturally and contributed to my own thinking, rather than as an alternative to my own thinking. However, the choice not to pursue either of these possibilities left me all the more aware of what different accounts either of these two educators, with their very distinctive approaches, would have come up with if they had been me, in this classroom, studying these two children's learning.

I realized that there are *bound* to be differences in the meanings that dif-ferent people find in the same evidence because the resources and perspec-tives which they bring to bear on the data are different. All of us have our own personal knowledge base, values, beliefs and assumptions derived from experience, training, reading and simply living in the world. We use these resources, together with the material of classroom experience, to help us make sense of what is happening and work out what we can do to support children's learning. They are what, for each of us, makes meaning-making possible. But because, for each of us, the content is different, inevitably the meaning that we construct based on the same evidence will inevitably differ. What we 'see', and what we are capable of seeing at a given point, depends not just upon what is actually *there* but upon the thinking that we bring to bear on what is there, and the knowledge, expectations and values that inform our thinking and hence seeing (Abercrombie, 1960). For the same reason, the accounts that I would have come up with a few years earlier or later would also have been different, because I would have had different resources of knowledge and experience to bring to the task, even if my purposes and everything else remained the same. A while after completing my analysis of Adrian's learning, for example, I came across the work of Carol Fox (1993) in which she explores the 'narrative competences' of young children derived from listening to stories read aloud. She shows how they embody knowledge derived in this way in their own original stories, told aloud, long before they have learnt to read or write. The book provides a framework and set of concepts which has many parallels with my analysis of Adrian's use of television literacy as a source of compositional knowledge. Had it been available at the time, I would no doubt have made use of it to help me to generate a vocabulary with which to analyse and describe his writing. In that case, my account of his learning would certainly have been different, and the learning occasioned by it for me would equally, no doubt, have been more directly influenced by the framework she proposes.

Even on this occasion, the accounts might have turned out differently if I had made choices differently at particular points in the analysis, and hence chosen different paths to pursue. For example, Annette's repertoire-writing strategy set off a train of thought about learning styles, an area which I was interested in but found highly problematic for all sorts of reasons. I started wondering if perhaps Annette's response to the conditions of the writing workshop was highlighting the need for a richer, more flexible and context-based understanding of individual learning styles. Had I pursued this possibility, the insights arrived at and conclusions reached would have been different, as would no doubt the implications for practice that would have been drawn out.

I chose not to pursue it because there seemed to be a more important set of issues to pursue relating to Annette's sense of herself and the radical changes which this self-concept appeared to have undergone – to judge from changes in her behaviour – during the course of just a few months. This decision was no doubt also influenced by recent reading I had done (e.g. Davies, 1989), which had highlighted the issue of identity – or rather *identities* – arguing that identities are not fixed but continually being reconstructed and renegotiated by individuals as they 'position' themselves within the range of opportunities available to them.

I concluded that it is inevitable that the same evidence will lend itself to differing interpretations and conclusions, and these differing outcomes need not necessarily be regarded as being in competition with one another. There is no reason to suppose that a situation rich in potential for yielding new ideas and possibilities for practice has only *one* legitimate set of insights to be opened up at a given moment for a particular child. Moreover, agreement between people about the meaning of a situation does not necessarily make it more likely that a judgement is sound. In my study of Adrian, for example, all the adults in the situation shared a common view of the limitations of his dialogue-writing. Consensus here may have been unhelpful from Adrian's point of view, because it reinforced the view that the limitation lay in Adrian's understanding, not ours, even though Adrian persistently complained that 'no-one understood' what he was trying to achieve with his writing. Consensus made it less likely that we would each question our individual interpretations, or open up to examination the shared norms implicitly structuring our thinking and leading us to construct the meaning of Adrian's learning in similar ways.

The work of Shirley Brice Heath (1983) provides a further telling illustration. Heath spent several years living and working with the communities whose language practices she studied, and then used the material generated to stimulate discussion with teachers about the implications for children's learning in school. Her work draws attention to differences in the language and literacy practices that teachers would not be in a position to discover for themselves, and provides a salutory insight into the impact that cultural and linguistic differences between teachers and children may have for children's development as learners and the identities which they acquire in school.

For example, one group of children had virtually no pre-school experience of answering certain kinds of questions, and so appeared to be very lacking linguistically as a result of an inability to 'answer simple questions'. On the other hand, they had a great deal of experience of the use of analogies in their interactions, a linguistic skill which teachers did not expect or call on, and so did not discover the children's abilities in this area. The perception of these children as having limited linguistic resources was generally shared by teachers who shared the same cultural and linguistic backgrounds, and so agreement might work in a way that was directly unhelpful to children, by serving to confirm the deficiency view and leave the underlying assumptions unexamined.

The example highlights the important responsibility which teachers have to guard against interpretations which leave us with a perception of children's learning as deficient because crucial aspects of the situation have been left unexamined. Where implicit norms are shared, an exchange of perspectives will not necessarily bring these to light and open them up to examination.

More fundamental, then, than whether there is agreement or disagreement about meanings is the question of whether the thinking upon which a particular interpretation relies has been *examined* or remains largely *unexamined*. Re-examining the different and sometimes conflicting interpretations that I had found myself making of the evidence collected in the course of my two studies, I realized that differing perspectives on the same situation differed in the sense of what they examined and what they left unexamined. An adequate analysis would need to have taken account of all these perspectives, if important dimensions of the situation were not to be overlooked and possibilities associated with them left unexplored. I concluded that there would be good reason to have confidence in hypotheses derived from our analysis if we knew that no essential aspect of the situation had been left unexamined.

The questioning framework outlined in Chapter 1 (see pp. 2–9) represents a first attempt to derive, from the experience of the research, a map of these essential dimensions of the analysis. Though I do not claim that this is necessarily a definitive framework, it does seem that our thinking would need to take account of the following:

- the relationship between children's learning and behaviour and features of the classroom and overall school context;
- how the teacher's particular resources, beliefs and values shape the meanings constructed from the evidence;
- the child's own meanings, purposes, feelings and agendas;
- how the teacher's own feelings affect the meanings bestowed on the situation;
- how the inescapable limitations of the information and resources which the teacher currently has available affect these meanings.

Confidence in the sound basis of the insights emerging from this process depends upon the kinds of thinking that has been done in the course of the analysis, and the extent to which our own thinking has been subjected to examination from different points of view. New insights provide a sound basis for action now – even if subsequent experience leads us to adjust our thinking – if the understandings reflected in them have been reached through a process which has attempted to open up our thinking about the situation from each of the five perspectives identified in the framework.

For example, when I found myself leaning towards an interpretation of Adrian's spelling which suggested that, contrary to my initial perception, all was proceeding well, I took steps to explore whether what might lead me to feel justified in this interpretation was actually a limitation in my existing understandings. I returned to the literature on dyslexia in order to see if I might be missing something important. Although my reading did not convince me to pursue this avenue on this occasion, the knowledge that I had considered and checked out an alternative perspective did allow me to feel greater confidence in my conclusions than if I had simply accepted them without further question. To have examined alternatives and made a considered decision between them not only increases the confidence that we can have in our decisions, but also creates a reservoir of possibilities that we can go back to and review, at any point, in the light of new experience and new resources becoming available.

This way of establishing criteria for judgement is consistent with the acknowledgement that no reading of a situation can claim certainty, or to be the one 'best' rendering of the evidence. It is consistent with the knowledge that our understanding is always incomplete, because there is always more to learn about any child or situation, and because no analysis we can ever make (however much time we have available) will ever be exhaustive. There will always be possibilities that have not yet occurred to us, or that other people might see because they would have a different set of personal resources and perspectives with which to construct new understandings. There is no one 'right' answer to the question for what might be done to further support the learning of any child.

To accept that any situation can yield a multiplicity of meanings and insights that suggest new possibilities for practice is not to retreat into relativism. It is not tantamount to saying that just *any* insight can be assumed to be sound, if it can be justified by the 'evidence'. I have argued that, in children's interests, we must be able to distinguish between conclusions that are, and those that are not, soundly based, and that the basis for making this distinction lies in the kinds of questioning to which our thinking has been submitted in reaching these conclusions.

MOVING BEYOND EXISTING THINKING

The framework for analysis which the research enabled me to identify has an in-built self-checking capacity which not only allows us to have confidence in the soundness of new ideas, but also provides in-built potential for learning. The five questioning moves help us to *move beyond* what we already think and know about the situation by probing what has not so far been examined within our *existing* thinking about the situation. The continual process of questioning existing interpretations from a variety of perspectives *is* what moves thinking on.

To recall, the five 'moves' are as follows

- Making connections: This move involves exploring how the specific characteristics of the child's response might be linked to features of the immediate and wider context. We ask ourselves: 'What might be helping to produce this response?'
- Contradicting: This move involves teasing out the underlying norms and assumptions that lead us to perceive the child's response as problematic. It asks: 'How else might this response be understood?' It seeks to uncover the norms and assumptions underlying a judgement, so that these can be reviewed and evaluated.
- Taking a child's eye view: This move involves trying to enter the child's frame of reference and see the meaning and logic of the child's response from the child's perspective. It asks: 'What meaning and purpose does this activity have for the child?'

- Noting the impact of feelings: This move involves examining the part that our own feelings are playing in the meaning we bestow on the situation, and in leading us to arrive at a particular interpretation. It asks: 'How do I feel about this?' and 'What do these feelings tell me about what is going on here?'
- Suspending judgement: This move involves recognizing that we may lack information or resources to have confidence in our judgements, and therefore holding back from making judgements about the child's needs while we take steps to add to our resources.

It was from the *process* of producing my accounts of Adrian's and Annette's learning that these ideas were derived, and so the accounts themselves cannot provide a complete illustration of how they helped to sustain the analysis and foster the development of thinking in the context of the research. Nevertheless, their influence can still be seen explicitly at many points throughout the accounts, and reference to these can therefore provide some further means of illustrating the thinking processes involved.

Virtually the whole of Annette's account is, in effect, an illustration of the questioning move that involves 'taking a child's eye view'. I used this to try to gain new insight into her progress over the period of the study, and resolve my own uncertainties about this by looking at the meaning from her point of view. Re-reading the evidence from this perspective helped to open up a great deal of unexamined thinking in interpretations I had made earlier, and suggested new ways of seeing the same material that would not otherwise have occurred to me.

Adrian's story is predominantly an illustration of the move that involves 'suspending judgement', while meanwhile taking necessary steps to acquire the information and resources that are felt to be needed. I realized that I could not follow through my research intentions of exploring how Adrian's development was bound up with the features of the writing workshop, until I had developed the necessary resources to *name, describe and understand* his development. Since I found no ready-made help in the literature, the study became a process of allowing myself to be taught by Adrian what needed to be understood about his writing and how it might be named and described.

Both stories also provide concrete illustration of the other moves in operation. The process of 'making connections' is constantly in evidence in both studies, since the whole purpose of the analysis was to try to understand how the children's activities and progress were bound up with features of the writing workshop. Other connections, though, were also continually being explored. The connection between the children's writing development and relationships with the peer group was central to my understanding of both children's learning, although it played a different part in each case. In Annette's case, I was aware of the problems she was experiencing in her relationships with other children, but it did not occur to me for a long time to make a connection between this aspect of her experience and the pattern of her writing development. When I suddenly saw a possible connection, it shed a whole new light on the meaning of her progress. The process of making connections, then, is not concerned with the connections we have *already* made, or which already inform our understanding of the child or situation. It is concerned with enabling us to make *new* connections, that will suggest new possibilities not previously thought of for supporting and enhancing the child's learning.

The move that involves 'contradicting' an existing interpretation, by considering other ways that the same situation could be read or understood, is also in evidence at a number of points in both stories. At the end of Annette's story, for instance, when I was still unsure about the conclusions that I seemed to be reaching, I used the work of Graves to contradict the view that all was not well with her repertoire-writing strategy. I forced myself to acknowledge and consider an alternative reading of the evidence, according to which Annette's progress might be seen as entirely consistent and appropriate for her stage of development. Although I still chose the more ambiguous reading, I had greater confidence in this choice knowing that it had been made as a result of a considered choice between alternatives.

As a result of developing the framework, I discovered that the move which involves 'noting the impact of feelings' is the one that I use least spontaneously myself in probing and questioning my own thinking, even though at a rational level I believe it to be really important. It was not even in the framework to start with, although once it had occurred to me I could indeed recognize how my feelings had been subtly influencing my interpretations throughout the analysis, and how they tried to lure me in particular directions which I then had to counteract via the other moves. The only explicit place where I recognized how feelings may affect how we read others' behaviour was at the end of Annette's story where it suddenly struck me that perhaps I had been attributing to her motivations and feelings that were in fact a projection of my own.

This realization, perhaps more than anything, convinces me of the importance of acknowledging that all interpretations have their unexamined elements. Therefore we need to have some means of systematically opening up to examination how these unexamined elements are shaping our perceptions and understandings. It is particularly important in the case of children whose learning gives cause for concern. A concern, by definition, means that something is worrying us about the child's learning. Yet the reading of the situation that is prompting our 'worry' will be subject to all the same influences, uncertainties and unexamined elements that have been discussed in this chapter and the previous one. We have a *responsibility*, therefore, to ensure that we do not leave important areas of our own thinking about the situation unexamined. When we exercise that responsibility by opening up our existing thinking to fresh examination, we also have at our disposal a powerful means of generating new insights that we can use to formulate new ideas for practice. This is the process that I have come to call 'innovative thinking'.

THE KNOWLEDGE BASE FOR INNOVATIVE THINKING

The five questioning moves are the means by which we marshall all our existing knowledge of the child, the situation and what makes a difference to children's learning in school contexts and use it to help generate new understandings and sound new hypotheses for the development of practice. Focusing the analysis on the dynamics of learning and teaching does not mean leaving aside consideration of wider social and contextual influences that we know have a bearing on children's responses to schooling, but are generally beyond our sphere of influence. It means using that knowledge differently: incorporating *into* the analysis awareness of those external influences to support our search for possibilities for the development of practice *within* the spheres over which we do have control. Although the power to generate new thinking does not depend upon access to new information or resources, this does not mean that we are sufficient unto ourselves or have no need to take into account the perspectives of others in reaching new understandings. On the contrary, our powers to understand and gain insight into new possibilities within the situation are greatly increased through contact with the ideas of others and the differing perspectives which they are able to bring. The knowledge base upon which we draw is largely dependent upon what we are able to acquire through experience, and we are dependent on others, therefore, for access to knowledge other than that which we can derive directly through our own experience.

In the last part of this chapter, I examine how the ideas and perspectives of others support, and can be incorporated into the process of innovative thinking, as an essential resource for our own thinking and to extend the possibilities that we are able to discover and exploit for ourselves. Significant others include the children themselves whose learning we seek to understand, their parents, families and carers, and the perspectives of communities served by the school. They include teacher colleagues and other educators, teachers with specialized knowledge and expertise and others who have an involvement in children's education.

The material of classroom experience provides a constant, and ever renewing source of new information to stimulate our thinking and generate new ideas and possibilities. However, it will never provide us with a vital insight into what children are like at home and outside school, which might shed a very different light on how they seem and how we perceive them in school. We need to create the means, therefore, to gain access to this alternative perspective, through dialogue with parents and children, in whatever ways are most convenient, economic of time and facilitative of the development of closer co-operation between home and school.

We need to create the means to extend our knowledge and understandings beyond our own cultural horizons, in order to understand and make full use of the cultural and linguistic resources of all pupils. Access to relevant literature and research has an important contribution to make in this area, as the work of Shirley Brice Heath ((1983, referred to above) and more recently that of Eve Gregory (1993a, 1993b) has admirably demonstrated.

Research which offers detailed insight into aspects of children's experience out of school can be important in helping teachers to gain a new appreciation of children's skills and abilities which are not so readily revealed in school contexts, and to revise misperceptions that come from lack of access to appropriate information. The work of Wells (1987), for instance, and Tizard and Hughes (1985) has drawn attention to differences in children's language use at home and at school, helping to illustrate the need to probe more searchingly into the impact of the school context on children's language, and what might be done to encourage children to use and develop their language abilities more fully in the school situation. Careful recording and comparison of parent–child interactions have helped to open up to re-examination assumptions about the linguistic deprivation of some children, and so raise expectations of their language capabilities on entry to school.

Access to research and literature helps, too, to ensure that in focusing on individual children we do not individualize the analysis, overlooking connections with features of the overall school context or wider social and political processes which help to shed light on a particular child's learning or behaviour. My study of Annette, for instance, ended by identifying – as one of the areas to work on – Annette's sense of the value of her own experience and what she has to write about. This could easily be treated as an individual problem of lack of confidence or self-esteem, overlooking (for instance) possible links with the value placed in the school curriculum on the learner's own prior experience and resources, links with the messages of value conveyed by the content, resources and methods of assessment used by a school, or links with wider social processes which tend to lead girls to devalue their ideas and abilities. Reading and research helps to heighten awareness of links that might not come to our notice simply through experience.

Having become aware, through the research, of my own limited use of the questioning move which takes note of the impact of feelings, I determined to draw on relevant sources in the literature to help strengthen my understanding of how feelings operate in the interpretive process, and what we can learn from developing a more conscious awareness in this area. I returned to the work of Salzberger-Wittenberg, Henry and Osborne (1983) and other sources to help me to think about how feelings about a child, a class, or ourselves affect the way that we read a situation; and also how the feelings that we experience in response to children may be a clue to the feelings being experienced by the children themselves. Work in the field of counselling is particularly helpful in this area, since the counsellor uses his or her own feelings constantly to try to tune into the experience of the client.

The knowledge base upon which we draw to support the functioning of the five interpretive moves is that which provides insight into the dynamics of teaching and learning in *any* situation. There is no reason to turn first, or predominantly, to specialist literature on learning difficulties and special needs which is shelved separately from the mainstream literature as if the latter had no specific relevance to the group of children conventionally referred to as having learning difficulties or special needs. Certainly, in recent years, more writers in the special needs field have been turning their attention to the mainstream literature as a source of insight into ways of enhancing learning for children perceived as experiencing difficulties (e.g. Ainscow and Tweddle, 1988; Ainscow, 1991; Booth, Potts and Swann 1987; Booth et al. 1992). However, we have not yet succeeded in exploiting the full power of the connection between the mainstream educational literature and the task of pursuing concerns about children's learning.

Once we have stopped thinking in terms of trying to diagnose difficulties or identifying unique, individual needs that require some sort of additional provision that other children do not require, it becomes much easier to recognize the relevance of the mainstream literature and pursue its possibilities more rigorously and systematically. There is, for example, a vast reservoir of untapped potential in the fields of social psychology, sociology, anthropology, feminist theory, linguistics, curriculum theory, learning theory and developments in thinking and pedagogy in the subject disciplines.

This is not to suggest that the existing 'specialist' literature ceases to have relevance. My aim in this book is to make a case for *widening* the range of resources that are thought to be relevant and thus given appropriate consideration in pursuing concerns about children's learning, not to make a case for closing off one source of insight in order to promote an alternative. The ideas of others, from whatever source, are needed to power our thinking processes and help to ensure that we do not overlook opportunities available to us for enhancing children's learning. The point of drawing on this literature is not to substitute for our own thinking but to increase our own *power* to think innovatively: to consider alternative possibilities and generate new ideas for translating insights thus derived into soundly-based strategies for practice.

In a similar vein, making the main focus of attention a search for unexamined possibilities within mainstream schools and classrooms does not exclude or make redundant the contribution of colleagues with specialist training and expertise in particular areas. If a blind child or newly arrived bilingual child becomes part of my class, I would welcome reassurance and support from someone with greater expertise than myself to help me initially in reaching understandings and making decisions about appropriate provision. If Adrian had been in my class, a teacher with knowledge of dyslexia might have been able to offer insights that I was unable to achieve myself and suggest possibilities that I could incorporate into my teaching that would not otherwise have come to my attention. These insights would not substitute for my own thinking and understanding of the situation; it would not replace an analysis of all the other features of the situation that need to be taken into account. It would provide an *additional* resource and stimulus for my own thinking that experience alone could not provide, and so increase the range of possibilities and strategies that I was able to generate for myself.

A CONTINUING PROCESS

The framework of moves allows us to have confidence in using the insights deriving from our analysis as a basis for action, while recognizing the tentative and open-ended nature of the understanding that supports them. It allows us to distinguish between understandings which do and which do not provide a sound basis for action, without closing off the potential for new learning associated with any judgement. There is always scope for returning to a prior analysis and reviewing it in the light of further experience or contact with the ideas of others. Possibilities that were previously excluded may suddenly seem relevant; resources that were not tapped on previous occasions may now be seen to have insights to provide. Discussion with others may enable us to see possibilities that previously passed unnoticed.

To revise our understandings in this way in the light of further experience is not to imply that we have discovered, after all, that they were not soundly based. Their 'sound basis' lay in the characteristics of the thinking process through which they were reached, not the finality of the outcomes. Uncertainty is an inherent and inescapable feature of teaching. Yet this knowledge need not undermine our confidence; on the contrary, it provides us with continual grounds for optimism. If there is no certainty, there are always grounds for hope that teachers can use their expertise to influence and change a situation that is causing concern. There is always room for further learning: for teachers to use their close knowledge of particular children and particular situations, and the complex dynamics of learning and teaching, to reach out for new insights which will help to unlock children's learning powers and enable them to use and develop them more fully.

7

Innovative Thinking and the Code of Practice

In the last two chapters, I have explained how the research led me to question my original focus on general curriculum development as a principal strategy for pursuing concerns about children's learning. The difficulties encountered in making sense of Annette's and Adrian's learning drew my attention to an important area of classroom experience – teachers' understandings of individual children's learning – which would not necessarily be touched by the broad developments in curricula that I was envisaging, yet which nevertheless had important consequences for children's development. They convinced me of the need to reinstate close study of the dynamics associated with individual children's learning as an integral and essential part of the task of pursuing concerns about children's learning. This could help to ensure that we do not overlook small-scale but significant possibilities for developing thinking and practice which could readily and easily be incorporated into teachers' existing classroom work. The two stories confirm that a highly individualized analysis need not divert attention away from wider possibilities for development within the overall curriculum and organization of classroom or school. What makes the difference is not whether the analysis is individualized or generalized, but the nature of the *thinking* that we bring to bear in either case: the questions that we do, or do not, ask ourselves in the process of seeking out new understandings and finding new ways forward.

These developments in my perception of the overall task happened to coincide with the publication of the first draft of the new *Code of Practice on the Identification and Assessment of Special Educational Needs* (DfE, 1994). A few years earlier, I would have been in complete despair about the guidance given, because all the focus was on individuals and individualized provision, with no mention made at all of any possibility – or need – for addressing concerns about children's learning through general developments in teaching, or in the overall curriculum and organization of the school. As a result of the new ideas emerging from the research, however, I was able to view the recommendations in a somewhat different light. I began to see the potential for responding to them in a way that was not a *retreat from* but a *development* of the thinking that had led me to reject a narrow focus on individuals and pursue instead a focus on general curriculum development as the principal task for support.

In this chapter, I summarize what is distinctive about the process of analysis proposed in this book, and explain why I believe that – when focused on individual children – it is not subject to the same limitations as other individualized approaches. I explain why I have confidence that it is feasible for busy teachers to incorporate thinking of this kind into their everyday work. I examine how the recommendations of the new Code of Practice could be fulfilled through an approach based on innovative thinking, and draw out the implications for the development of a whole-school approach, including the use of additional resources and the place and role of support teachers.

A 'NEW' APPROACH?

When a child's learning triggers concern and a desire to intervene in some way to facilitate development, there are different ways in which we can set about the task. Which we choose to guide and structure our thinking is important because our choice will shape the questions that we ask and the possibilities that we consider. It will determine the extent to which we consider possibilities within mainstream education to be relevant to the task of pursuing concerns about children's learning.

One approach, which I shall call 'diagnostic' thinking (see Figure 7.1) is to look for something *wrong* that can be put right: some deficiency in the child's functioning or prior experience, or in the current learning environment. The idea is that if we can establish, or *diagnose*, the *source of the problem*, this will tell us, or at least point towards, what might be done to *remedy* it, compensate for it, or reduce the extent of its impact on the child's learning. It may also help us to realize action that might be taken to *prevent* its occurrence in the future.

1. *Diagnostic thinking*	2. *Differential thinking*	3. *Innovative thinking*
• diagnose	• assess	• analyse, probe
• learning difficulties	• needs	• unexplored possibilities
• causes/sources	• identification	
• remedies	• individual/special	• new insight
• compensatory strategies	• match	• power
• prevention	• provision/resources	• potential
	• differentiation	• making a difference

Figure 7.1

A second approach, which I call 'differential thinking', is to look for ways to *match provision* more closely to the child's individual *needs* and personal learning styles. If a child does not seem to be responding as we hope or expect to our teaching, this is taken as an indication that he or she may have specific needs that are not yet being adequately met in the current situation. If we can *identify* those needs through careful *assessment*, this will tell us what provision needs to be made available to the child in order to facilitate more successful learning.

Both these first two approaches reflect a fundamentally positive stance on the part of those who adopt them. They start from an assumption that there *is* potential for enhancing children's learning to be found if we actively seek it out, and a commitment to finding ways of exploiting it in the interests of learners. However, the kinds of thinking they encourage may well leave much of the potential that exists within mainstream education unexplored. Because the focus is upon the *child*, there is no guarantee that the analysis will open up to examination and reconsideration all, or indeed any, of the aspects of the situation – and practitioners' thinking – wherein that potential lies.

In the first case, the analysis of causes and contributory factors may include a consideration of the impact of the learning context on the child's learning, but leave unexamined our perception that the child is experiencing difficulties and the particular terms in which those difficulties are formulated. It will lead us to consider possibilities within our own classrooms and schools only to the extent that we believe that some aspect of school experience might be contributing to the child's difficulties, or might provide a solution to a diagnosed difficulty arising from another source. If our attempts to explain and identify causes lead to the identification of factors largely beyond our power to influence, then this is likely to diminish our sense of the value of pursuing possibilities in the immediate situation, because these seem to be merely cosmetic as long as the causes continue to exert their influence and remain unaddressed.

In the second case, our search for what is distinctive about the child's individual learning needs may lead us to concentrate on identifying and describing characteristics of the child's learning, without recognizing that these perceived 'characteristics' are not objectively existing attributes of the child but products of the situation, in two senses. They are products of the child's encounter with learning experiences previously provided, and so need to be understood as the child's response to that situation. They are also products of our own meaning-making, and so are contingent upon the particular understandings and resources that we bring to the interpretive task. A programme of work to address a concern about children's learning may have limited impact if it leaves unexamined most of the features of the situation that were contributing to the identification of the child's learning as an occasion for concern. This is likely to be demoralizing for the teacher, who has put in considerable work to develop the programme, and also for the child. It may well discourage the teacher from further effort, either believing current levels of attainment reflect the child's ceiling of ability, or assuming that one-to-one support or specialist attention is needed to help the child.

This book has proposed a third way of thinking about and pursuing concerns about children's learning. Innovative thinking involves searching out new possibilities for responding to a situation – or child's learning – that is causing concern through a probing *analysis* of our *existing* thinking and understandings. It involves going to work on our existing thinking in such a way as to generate *new* insight into what might be done, *beyond* what is currently being done or tried, to support and enhance the child's learning.

Innovative thinking can be used both to pursue concerns about individual children and to pursue concerns formulated in a more generalized way and which apply to considerable numbers of children. At an individual level, it allows the analysis to stay focused on the specific characteristics of individual children's learning, while providing a means for systematically reviewing ways of understanding these characteristic *other than* as a reflection of personal characteristics and limitations. It ensures that perceptions of children's learning that prompt concern are carefully questioned, rather than simply taken for granted in the terms in which they were originally formulated (e.g 'Annette's writing seems to have lost some of the positive qualities which it showed a few months ago.'). Through the analysis, the concern itself is progressively transformed into new hypotheses about what might be done – that is not currently being done – to support the child's learning, grounded in a developing understanding of the situation.

At the more generalized level, innovative thinking involves generating new ideas in a similar way, but with reference to a category or group of children who share a common characteristic – say, limited literacy skills – or a concern that affects many children – such as truancy or disaffection. It involves processing available information, experience and literature in such a way as to achieve new insights and understandings in which to ground hypotheses about what might be done to support and enhance learning, and as part of a programme of development work intended to benefit all children.

The approach can be used by teachers working on their own initiative – for instance, a teacher deciding to try out some ideas with the whole class for encouraging readers' more active engagement with texts (Lunzer and Gardner, 1979). It can also be used by teachers working together to address an issue of shared concern. For example, without referring to specific details of any group of children transferring from primary school, we know from experience that there are always a significant number of children who do not have very advanced literacy skills. Teachers can use the insights drawn from previous experience of working with children with limited literacy, together with insights drawn from research, reading, visits, INSET, etc. to generate new ideas and possibilities that might be introduced into their future teaching in order to ensure the fullest possible participation and involvement of all children. They do not need to wait until encountering particular individuals and then attempt to analyse and tackle their difficulties on an individual-by-individual basis. Such work can be undertaken as part of the school's on-going programme of development work, and can often provide a stimulus to whole-curriculum developments from which all children can benefit.

The category 'children with limited literacy' operates as a standpoint from which to probe as yet untried or unthought of possibilities within the mainstream curriculum and, as with the individual analysis, may open up new ideas and strategies which are either specific to the identified group or of more general relevance. Other categories can also operate in this way. Any school population will or might include children with partial sight or hearing, bilingual children, traveller children, refugee children, bereaved children and so on. Each provides a standpoint from which to see new possibilities for supporting and enhancing learning that might not otherwise come to our attention. Each has the potential to prompt fresh thinking and open up insights not just of relevance to the distinct group but to all children.

What my study helped to do was to highlight the limitations of an approach based on generalized thinking and show how and why it needs to be set alongside – though not replaced – by individualized thinking. Annette's and Adrian's stories illustrate how the two kinds of thinking connect up, because individualized thinking provides one important source of ideas that can, if we choose, be introduced into our work with children more generally. In both cases, relevant resources (from experience, contact with others, research, reading etc.) are brought together with the material of classroom experience to generate ideas about what might be done that is not currently being done to enhance learning opportunities for children individually and/or collectively. Teachers work out how to incorporate into practice the developmental possibilities they have come up with, interpret the children's responses to these in the manner described to gauge their effectiveness, and decide on further action based on the new understanding that emerges.

TIME FOR INNOVATIVE THINKING?

As the two stories illustrate, most of the ideas emerging from the analysis – even in the context of the research – could easily be incorporated into a teacher's on-going work with the class. Since there is no prescriptive relationship between any new insights generated and how the teacher chooses to respond to these in practice, the teacher makes the choice about whether to use them to inform her one-to-one interactions with the child or whether to incorporate them into planned work for the group as a whole. In many cases, what emerges is a changed perspective on the situation and new questions to think about rather than ideas requiring a specific, and time-consuming, response.

The time needed for an approach based on innovative thinking, when focused at an individual level, is therefore mainly time to do the thinking. It does not depend on teachers having time to implement individualized programmes of work. Time for thinking is, of course, always at a premium. Nevertheless, the ordinary circumstances of practice do include at least some time for thinking about individuals and working with individuals on a one-to-one basis. Even in the midst of practice, the framework can provide an ever-present reminder that there are many possible angles from which we might view the significance of the child's activity, and helps alert us to those which we might be overlooking. Of course, we cannot stop to deliberate all the possibilities, but we can use the framework as a structure and support for the processes of reflection and planning which we would do anyway, and particularly to inform future plans regarding particular children whose learning is of concern.

An ordinary teaching week also includes time spent in reviewing and reflecting upon what happened in the course of a day and using the ideas emerging to inform future teaching plans. In my experience, teachers often also spend a considerable amount of time thinking and worrying about what to do in response to children whose learning or behaviour concerns them. Sometimes we find ourselves going over and over in our minds incidents which have caused a sense of stress, disappointment or professional failure.

Innovative thinking describes how we can take control of the situation and use whatever time we have available as constructively as possible to identify possible ways forward. The framework is designed to help structure our thinking and prompt us into asking questions that might otherwise not occur to us. Without underestimating the many constraints which limit teachers' freedom of manoeuvre, it ensures that our available resources are always invested in a search for possibilities that we are in a position to pursue ourselves. It means that we need never be at the mercy of a situation that is causing concern and distress, because we always have at our disposal a practical means to help open up the situation and search out previously unthought of possibilities for influencing and changing some aspect of the situation through the use of our existing resources.

My central argument, then, in making my case that innovative thinking can be incorporated into teachers' ordinary everyday work, is that it does not imply finding *more* time, but using whatever time we *do* have available differently. The fact that the criteria for judging the soundness of new ideas do not depend upon the depth or exhaustiveness of the analysis means that there is no reason why the process of innovative thinking cannot be scaled down to a form that can be incorporated into teachers' ordinary everyday work. Just a little bit of thinking is enough to generate sound new ideas to guide practice, as long as steps have been taken to open up our thinking about the situation from every angle.

For example, the teachers who worked with Shirley Brice Heath, in the study described in the previous chapter, would have been able to open up for themselves some of the issues that her work drew their attention to if they had automatically made use of innovative thinking in response to their concerns about children's difficulties in 'answering simple questions'. They could have immediately started asking themselves questions about this perception: about what counts as a 'simple' question ('contradicting'), what kinds of questions they routinely ask children and what other kinds of questions they might ask which children would show themselves to be able to answer ('making connections'). They might have probed a bit further into what sense the questions make from the child's point of view, how familiar children are with questions of this kind in their own prior experience ('taking a child's eye view'), and indeed what other kinds of questions children are more used to asking and responding to in their family environment ('making connections from a child's eye view'). Such questions do not take much time to ask, but they do begin to open up new optimistic horizons of possibility in place of the gloomy prognosis of a life-time of low attainment which might otherwise be attached to the perception that 'they cannot even answer the simplest question'.They suggest possibilities for further enquiry ('suspending judgement'), once teachers have recognized the need for more information about the kinds of language which children most frequently use at home and how these differ from those used at school.

I believe that teachers will also be more inclined to *commit* time to innovative thinking, if they are convinced that possibilities are there to be found, if they are confident that they know how to set out finding them themselves, and if they believe that the investment of time will potentially be of benefit to all children. I have proposed innovative thinking as a process and procedure to support teachers in using their thinking powers in this way. I have argued that the questions which make up the framework are questions which most teachers already use anyway to seek out ways of influencing and enhancing learning within their everyday teaching. All that the framework does is to make those ways of thinking explicit and show how they can be used together to create a developmental tool for moving thinking forward.

Indeed, it could be argued that morally we do not have a choice. If our experience and understandings of children's learning lead us to experience concern about particular individuals – now to be formally recorded in a register of concern – we owe it to the child to examine carefully the dynamics of the situation giving rise to the concern. We must be careful not to overlook contextual influences shaping the child's learning, and also not to overlook influences on our own thinking that are leading us to identify this learning as an occasion for concern. If we accept that what we 'see', and are capable of seeing, depends not just upon what is *there* but the resources that we bring to the task, then what we see as a matter for concern is also inevitably linked to our own thinking in the same way. When we exercise our *responsibility* towards children by exploring the dynamics of the situation helping to produce our sense of concern, the thinking that we do becomes the source of our own power to influence and change the situation that is causing concern – or our perception of it – through the use of our existing resources.

THE CODE OF PRACTICE

Innovative thinking can be used by any teacher in any situation. However, many of the possibilities that may arise through this thinking – say, for a change in grouping practices, or for more fruitful contact with parents and communities – can only be pursued in practice if agreement is reached at a whole-school, year or departmental level. Now that all schools are required to have a clear policy for meeting special educational needs, there is a legal framework supporting the development of practice on a whole-school basis. In formulating policy, schools are required to 'have regard' to the *Code of Practice on the Identification and Assessment of Special Educational Needs*. There is no obligation on schools to follow the advice and procedures laid down in the Code to the letter, only to be able to justify whatever procedures they have chosen to adopt as enabling them to fulfil their statutory and professional responsibilities to children whose learning gives cause for concern.

The Code lays down a five-stage process of assessment, leading towards a formal statement of special educational needs, of which the first three are mainstream school-based. These stages represent a set of progressive steps and measures which schools should undertake themselves in order to foster children's fullest possible participation in and progress within the mainstream curriculum. Recent discussions with teachers suggest that many fear that the massive increase in paper work entailed in documenting this work for each child will have an impact on schools' work that is more bureaucratic than pedagogic. Indeed, in my experience, many practitioners fear that the record-keeping aspects will absorb the energy that could otherwise be put into developments of teaching.

Built into the staged assessment process is also a gradual handing over of responsibility for doing the thinking about children's learning from mainstream teachers to the special needs co-ordinator. This perpetuates the old message that more specialized knowledge and expertise is needed to identify and meet the needs of some children, even if part of the intention is to alleviate the burden on the mainstream teacher who has twenty-nine or more other children to provide for. The focus at all stages is on individual children, and there is only passing reference to the need to see special needs in the context of schools' overall organization and practices. This reads as a warning not to overlook the possibility that schools can cause or exacerbate special needs. It therefore casts the potential that exists within mainstream education in negative terms and, as I have argued, limits our sense of the scope available to us for enhancing learning and achievement to areas of practice thought to be contributing to a problem.

There is no reference at all to the possibility that general developments in teaching might have a valuable part to play in supporting individual learning needs, and therefore that efforts to support individual children's learning could at the same time potentially benefit all children. Nor is there any reference to the potential for drawing out the general lessons from past work with individual children, as well as insights drawn from research or reading, to inform developments of teaching for future groups of children. Only if these more general dimensions of the work are being undertaken alongside work to support individual children can the support for individual children itself achieve manageable proportions and serve rather than substitute for the longer-term view.

Most importantly, perhaps, schools could, with monumental effort, fulfil all the suggestions of the Code of Practice to the letter, yet still not ask the kinds of questions which *need* to be asked in order to ensure that all relevant aspects of the situation giving rise to the concern have been taken into account. We could do all this information-gathering, record-keeping and individual planning and review, yet overlook the real sources of our power to make a difference to children's learning.

I believe that in developing responses to the Code of Practice, we need to start from our existing understanding of what can and needs to be done to support and enhance the learning of children whose work or behaviour gives cause for concern. The requirement to 'have regard to the Code' then becomes a self-checking device helping to ensure that the measures we are proposing to take do match the requirements at the level of principle, if not procedure, and that nothing essential has been inadvertently overlooked. Starting from existing understanding means, for me, *making thinking central*. It means making sure that, in arriving at any judgements about what needs to be done in response to concerns about children's learning, we have opened up our thinking to examination from all relevant points of view.

The function of a whole-school policy would be to set in place the structures and conditions that would help to ensure that possibilities for enhancing learning within existing (whole-school or individual class) arrangements that *could* be exploited *are* indeed recognized and exploited (to the extent that this is feasible within constraints of time and resources). The school-based phase of the staged assessment process would thus be concerned with a gradual intensification of the search for (as yet) unexploited possibilities within the school and classroom situation where a particular child's learning was giving rise to concern.

Stage One would involve the child's teacher (or teachers) pursuing their concerns about the child's learning by going to work on his or her existing understandings, through the process of innovative thinking. Though the ideas have their source in the study of the distinctive characteristics of the child's response, the possibilities envisaged may not be limited to those individuals. Some indeed are individual-specific, but others will raise questions or suggest developments of a more general nature, and are most appropriately addressed at whole-class or whole-school level.

Stages Two and Three would involve probing more deeply, and with the increasing support of experienced colleagues, into the complex dynamics at work in the situation, and using the feedback provided by possibilities previously tried by the class teacher herself to support and enhance the child's learning. It would be necessary to acknowledge and develop understanding of the many circumstances, in a busy classroom, that may prevent us from noticing and exploiting possibilities for development, even when we are actively seeking them out. These include, for example, the strategies which children devise to please teachers and demonstrate success, whose purpose is to obscure from teachers their lack of understanding and need for help.

Stage Four would be entered, not when all the possibilities had been exhausted (since there is no end to the potential for generating new understandings) but when those involved felt that further possibilities could not be identified or exploited without additional resources (human or other) or felt that they had reached the limits of their collective resources for the time being without apparently significantly benefiting the child's learning. The case for statutory assessment would involve providing evidence of the adequacy of previous assessments made, of the outcomes of developmental possibilities pursued.

We do not need to make use of the language of 'earning difficulties and special needs in formulating a policy and whole-school approach based on innovative thinking, yet consistent with the Code's requirements. Throughout this book, I have systematically replaced all reference to the task of 'meeting special educational needs' with the task of pursuing concerns about children's learning. This is consistent with the Code's own terms, which propose that Stage One of the assessment process should be triggered by a concern. However, it would also serve to ensure that the *negative* terms in which concerns about children's learning are most often couched would fulfil a *positive* function in the analytic process: as the starting points which lead us towards new understandings, the resources which help us to generate new ideas about what we might further do, within the existing situation, to support and enhance a particular child's learning.

A WHOLE-SCHOOL APPROACH?

According to this interpretation, the staged assessment process would become stages in the development of teachers' *thinking*, probing progressively more deeply into the dynamics at work in that situation, and with increasing help from colleagues. A whole-school approach, consistent with the ideas in this book, would be designed to facilitate the maximum possible exercise and development of all teachers' powers of innovative thinking. This aim would be central in deciding how best to employ any additional resources, and care would be taken to use additional adult support in a way that helps to foster rather than substitute for the achievement of this main aim.

A priority task would be to work towards creating an ethos in which the ability to ask searching questions and to generate new possibilities is generally recognized as an expression of expertise rather than an admission of the shortcomings of existing practice. The idea that we ought to keep asking questions of our own thinking may seem threatening if we see it as something to be undertaken only in case we have got things wrong, rather than as an essential mode of professional thinking. Through the *exercise* of our expertise, in going to work on our thinking, we discover how we might further *apply* our expertise to support and enhance children's learning. The expertise is more like that of a detective who has no investment in existing thinking, except as a resource for moving thinking on, by bringing his or her knowledge and expertise to bear on the situation, and reaching out for new undestandings.

If an ethos of this kind can be established, then any available additional staff can join in the search for new possibilities, asking questions without fear of undermining colleagues or casting aspersions on their professional competence. Obviously, there would still be a need for trust and mutual respect to be built up in support partnerships, but this would be developed within an ethos which was already respectful of the complexity of the teaching task and recognized that no amount of experience, expertise and careful planning will enable us to predict with certainty what will engage and empower a particular child or group of children on a particular occasion.

The function of any additional adult support, then, in an approach based on innovative thinking would be primarily to *help in the quest for, imple-*

mentation and review of possibilities for enhancing children's learning. The preceding chapters have highlighted the complexity of the teacher's task and the many factors which may prevent teachers from noticing and exploiting possibilities for enhancing children's learning even when they are actively seeking them out. Consequently, much that *could* be done to enhance children's learning and achievements may *not* be done, because of the pressures of numbers or because teachers lack collaborative opportunities to support one another in generating and implementing innovative ideas. There is every reason, then, to provide as much additional support as possible in classrooms to assist teachers in using their power to exploit the possibilities available to them more fully.

If two teachers join forces in innovative thinking, whether they are building the lessons of past learning into general curriculum planning, or pooling understandings relating to a particular child, the different resources can potentially act as a stimulus to one another's thinking, opening up different possibilities and perspectives than either might consider alone. Such support may indeed be particularly important in the early stages of discovering the potential of the five questioning moves to open up new possibilities *beyond* teachers' existing thinking and practice for enhancing learning opportunities for children whose responses (or entitlements) give cause for concern.

Although the pressures on both support teachers and mainstream teachers are so great that there may not be much time for joint discussion and planning outside of lessons, it is important that the support teacher should be aware of the possibilities that the class teacher is currently pursuing and the thinking underpinning these so that the support teacher can offer feedback which will help to review that thinking and the ideas derived from it in an on-going way in the light of experience. This would give a clear practical purpose to the idea of an individual education plan: a quick and simple record of possibilities tried and how thinking evolved in the light of the child's response.

Support teachers engaging in such individual support could also be invited to feed generalizable insights arising from their work into general curriculum planning and development processes, since they may not be in a position to implement generalizable insights arising from innovative thinking themselves. In this way, the support teacher can manage the interface between the individual level and the generalized level of analysis and response, such that work at an individual level can still contribute to the generalized process, and not function simply as a substitute for the more fundamental rethinking of curricula that may be implied. It would be important, however, to emphasize that support teachers must submit their first impressions and interpretations to analysis just as rigorously as their mainstream colleagues, since it is all too easy for support teachers to find themselves engaging in pseudo-innovative thinking about other people's practice, and generating ideas for development that are simply their own unexamined taken-for-granted notions of 'good practice'.

Moreover, there would seem to be a useful function for support teachers in enabling mainstream teachers to have an opportunity to take the support role (preferably in their own classes) for part of lessons, on a regular basis, in order to study closely the experience of individual children and consider what untapped potential might be suggested by their observations. It would be important to emphasize (and test out through experience) that there is always scope for innovative thinking in any classroom, irrespective of teachers' individual expertise, because of the complex dynamics of classroom processes, the unpredictability of individual children's responses, and the inevitable limitations of our existing knowledge and resources. A corpus of collective knowledge and resources could thus gradually be built up by inviting teachers to share with colleagues their experience of innovative thinking and the outcomes of their efforts to build these ideas into their on-going work with children.

It would be one of the learning support co-ordinator's specific responsibilities to help teachers in doing the thinking that would lead to the discovery of new possibilities when the child does not seem to be responding to strategies already tried. If it is difficult to find time to see every teacher about every child, structures could be set in place, say, during directed twilight or INSET time for self-chosen pairs of teachers to meet together to discuss children about whom there is continuing concern, with the learning support co-ordinator circulating amongst pairs and, perhaps, in particular helping to translate ideas and insights emerging into strategies for practice.

Since the assumption is that mainstream teachers already have the expertise and knowledge to generate new thinking about a situation causing concern, the learning support teacher's role is not to provide the necessary expertise that others lack but to supplement and enrich the possibilities that others are able to see by virtue of her own experience and expertise. Just as research and literature has an important role to play in helping to increase our powers of innovative thinking, so too is there a place for specialist input without displacing or undermining teachers' own powers of thinking. I can use the knowledge, ideas and expertise of others in conjunction with my own experience and knowledge of the child to generate new ideas and possibilities for the development of practice that I might not have been able to come up with – or perhaps have confidence in – on my own. In my experience, what often happens in fact is that the outside expert provides expert confirmation for the legitimacy of the teacher's own ideas, rather than adding to the teacher's repertoire of specialist techniques, materials or insights.

Particular kinds of professional development and in-service education opportunities would be needed to support a whole-school approach designed to encourage innovative thinking. For example, there would be a need to provide opportunities to share and discuss with colleagues case studies of work with individual children, in order to share experience and strengthen conviction in the scope available for enhancing learning. There would also be a need to create opportunities to share and enrich the knowledge base upon which innovative thinking draws, especially in those areas where essential insights are less readily derived from experience.

The framework is designed to support the *process* of classroom analysis, but is not intended to prescribe or predetermine its content. Asking the five kinds of questions rigorously and systematically will ensure that we keep essential aspects of the situation that are easily overlooked under review. However, it cannot in itself guarantee that our analysis will take account of the important features, say, of the immediate or wider context which may be helping to shape the child's response, and which may be susceptible to influence, if we can gain insight into how the dynamics are operating in the case of a particular child. Part of the task of professional development and practitioner research, then, will be to build and extend the knowledge base we have available, so that we are able to see connections and open up possibilities that would otherwise have passed unnoticed.

If we have a clear sense of what needs to be done and why, in pursuing concerns about children's learning, then we need not necessarily be thrown off course by initiatives which at first sight seem to be requiring different ways of thinking and demanding different ways of using our energies and resources than those we believe to be in the best interests of children. The requirements upon schools relating to the Code of Practice can be turned to advantage, if we use our own understandings to guide the development of our responses, and interpret its requirements in these terms.

It is my belief that the enormously time-consuming and bureaucratic procedures envisaged by the Code would not be needed within a whole-school approach based on innovative thinking. They are a way to try to ensure that schools do take necessary steps prior to referral of a child, to ensure that whatever can be done within the immediate situation is done to smooth the child's path to learning. In this book, I have suggested that the steps proposed in the Code are not the only steps and have offered an alternative view of what schools might do instead in order to safeguard children's interests and open up these wider possibilities.

I would, however, want to preserve the Code's commitment to involve parents and children in contributing to the thinking that we do, ostensibly on their behalf, in order to provide enhanced learning and achievement. Although it may not be easy to gain access to, and hear, others' perceptions of the situation, it is vital to seek out that information to the extent that this is feasible within the usual constraints and pressures of teaching. A school policy needs to incorporate means by which teachers can draw on and use this knowledge to help understand the dynamics of a situation causing them concern and discover possibilities for supporting and enhancing learning which are dependent on these added insights. The learning support co-ordinator is not the only relevant person who might have responsibility for seeking out this information. It could be the form teacher or tutor who acts as the first point of contact and passes on what they have learnt to others who come into contact with the child.

I believe that it is vital for a whole-school approach to be built around teachers' use of their powers of innovative thinking because there is so much to learn about how school and classroom processes, including our own thinking and teaching, help to determine the extent and limits of each child's achievement. Moreover, it is teachers who are best placed to generate that new knowledge and understanding. What we already know (through experience and research) needs to be marshalled to support our attempts to understand how we can best intervene to support children's learning in individual cases. Each individual case also generates insights which contribute to the development of that more general understanding. When teachers use their powers of innovative thinking simultaneously both at an individual-responsive and at a general-developmental level, the task of pursuing concerns about children's learning provides a powerful impetus for enhancing the quality of education generally.

8

Innovative Thinking and Practitioner Research

In real life, things never quite work out to plan, and this study was no exception. My original intention had been to use the outcomes of the research to help decide how to develop my own future professional role. However, my research post was only a temporary one, so I had to make a decision about what to do next long before I had begun to see a way through all the new confusion and uncertainties that the study had opened up for me. I decided to move into in-service education, since this would allow me to be directly involved with teachers in exploring ideas relating to curriculum and teaching in a way that had been too infrequently possible in support work.

This move provided access to new experience which in turn had a significant impact on the outcomes of the research. It brought issues relating to practitioner research more to the forefront of my concerns, whereas previously I had seen the task simply in terms of justifying, on my own account, the methodological approach that I had chosen. Now, as a result of working with experienced teachers on enquiry-based in-service courses, I started to see connections between the methodological questions posed by my study and more general debates in the field of practitioner research. In particular, I realized that my study might be able to make a contribution to these debates, by helping to establish a clearer distinction between modes of practitioner research which require knowledge of research methodology and an approach where knowledge and expertise derived from teaching might be accepted as a legitimate and sufficient resource for research.

In this chaper, I explain the background to these ideas in more detail, and the questions I found myself asking as a result of the new experiences encountered through in-service work. I explain the contribution that innovative thinking may have to make to the area of practitioner research methodology, and what it has to add to other accounts of reflective practice already well-established in the field.

THE TEACHER-AS-RESEARCHER

When I took up my research post, I found that I was to have the opportunity of working on two projects (apart from my own study), not just one. One was a project studying the impact upon practice in schools of the changing role of support teachers. The other was a project studying the development of collaborative group work in primary schools. The experience of working on the collaborative group work project turned out to be very influential, quite by accident, on the development of the methodology for my own study.

At the time, I had no formal training in research methods, nor experience of research, other than small-scale development work, undertaken as part of in-service courses. The main resource which I was able to bring to both was direct experience of working in both these areas (although my experience of collaborative learning was at secondary level). While I was hastily reading up on research methods, and working out the more formal structure of the research, I set up some informal opportunities to observe and participate regularly in various classrooms where teachers were known to be committed to collaborative learning.

The experience led to a complete transformation of my understanding of collaborative learning that was in no way envisaged prior to the research (Hart, 1989b, 1992b). Moreover, I knew without a shadow of doubt that this transformation had come about simply by *being in the classrooms and thinking* with whatever resources I could muster, and not because of any careful research design, or the influence of the new knowledge that I was acquiring about research methodology.

What happened was that, to my surprise, I came across very little group work in the classrooms visited. To start with, other research colleagues and I explained this away in various ways, assuming that, if I kept looking, I would eventually find some. When I did not – or at least not as much, or in the form, that I was expecting – it occurred to me that perhaps I was looking for the wrong thing. There was plenty of collaborative learning going on, but it did not necessarily take the form of group work. The task, then, became one of drawing on the experience of these classrooms to find a way of conceptualizing the form which collaboration *did* take – if this was not mainly group work – and to investigate the processes that facilitated its development.

As a result of this experience, an idea began to take shape that perhaps the knowledge and skills which a teacher has already acquired through teaching can be *sufficient in themselves* for generating new knowledge and understanding, without necessarily needing to be underpinned by data collection techniques or informed by additional knowledge of research methodology. The process I had undergone certainly seemed to have much in common with Schon's (1983) account of reflective practice, as if I had simply applied in the context of research the same skills which, according to Schon, practitioners use in the context of their ordinary work: 'As [the practitioner] tries to make sense of [a surprising or puzzling phenomenon], he also reflects on the understandings that have been implicit in his action, understandings which he surfaces, criticises, restructures and embodies in further action' (p. 50). It seemed that what had happened was that the new situations encountered through the research had brought me up against the limits of my existing thinking. These limits were reflected in the experience of not being able to find the group work that the research had taken for granted would be found in classrooms where teachers were committed to collaborative learning. Exploring the mismatch between what I expected and what actually seemed to be going on in the name of collaborative learning in the classrooms visited provided a means of surfacing, re-examining and eventually moving beyond previous thinking in order to construct a more adequate understanding of the relationship between group work and collaborative learning. The new learning was brought about, it seemed, through the interplay between the thinking that I brought to the interpretive task and the demands made upon that thinking by the new situation. It did not seem to depend upon or require expertise beyond that which I had already acquired through teaching.

I determined to try and create conditions for my own study that would support a similarly transformative learning process. This seemed to imply claiming the right to use my resources as a teacher as a legitimate and sufficient basis for research. To be on the safe side, I did pay heed to advice in the literature on participant observation and data quality in planning my observations (e.g. McCall and Simmons, 1969), because I was not yet sure enough of my ground to risk not taking usual precautions. However, my hunch was that such precautions would not turn out to be of central significance in establishing the sound basis of any new learning that emerged.

I searched for support for this approach in the literature on practitioner research, but found it difficult to make straightforward connections. Most work in this field has been concerned with developing a methodology to support teachers in researching their *own* practice: one that is adapted to the natural cycle of action and reflection that teaching involves (e.g. Stenhouse, 1975; Winter, 1989; McNiff, 1988; Elliott, 1991). There are mixed messages, too, about need for and appropriate application of knowledge of research methods in practitioner inquiry. Since my study involved neither action, nor use of research techniques, and was carried out in other people's classrooms, it did not seem to fit readily into existing practitioner research traditions. Indeed, it was difficult even to claim it as practitioner research, since I was carrying out the research as an outsider, working full time in an institution of higher education, and not currently carrying out the professional role which had prompted the study.

Nevertheless, I felt that it could legitimately be seen as a form of practitioner research because the impetus for the work and its specific questions arose from my work as a support teacher. My aim in carrying out the study was to help me to make important decisions relating to my future professional work. In gaining access to this classroom, my function was not that of the traditional 'outsider' researcher who, by virtue of being an outsider, is able to illuminate the familiar, taken-for-granted practices of others. Rather it was a means of stepping outside my own immediate professional role in order to develop my own understandings from a fresh vantage point. It was my own work and the thinking that informed it that was to be the focus for examination and development. These teachers' and children's work simply provided the resource for evaluating, refining and reformulating my own.

I decided to continue to pursue the idea of my study as a (somewhat unorthodox) instance of practitioner research for two reasons. Firstly, there were a small number of practitioner studies which, like my own, were carried out (in whole or part) in other people's classrooms, and where the principal resource used was the authors' own insight as experienced teachers (e.g. Holt, 1969; Armstrong, 1980; Rowland, 1984). Secondly, my new experience of working on courses designed to help teachers acquire knowledge of research methodology was leading me to question if perhaps this additional knowledge might sometimes have an inhibiting rather than an enabling impact upon teachers' own powers of critical thinking.

It occurred to me that it might be helpful to try, through my study, to draw a clearer line of demarcation between modes of practitioner research which make use of conventional research methods and techniques for data collection and analysis, and those which acknowledge and use practitioners' own existing knowledge and expertise as a legitimate and sufficient resource for research. Then practitioners who, as in my case, preferred to rely on their own thinking, or felt encumbered by research methods, could legitimately choose to use their own resources without opening up their work to criticism as a substandard form of research.

In this case, research would be regarded as simply an extension of practice: an application of existing skills and expertise under new circumstances designed to facilitate reflection in particular ways. Armstrong (1981, p. 16) explains his understanding of the relationship between research and teaching in similar terms: 'It [the research] seeks to capitalise on teachers' diagnostic and analytical skills by providing them with an opportunity to achieve greater detachment, a closer scrutiny and a more precise speculation of their pupils' thought and action than circumstances generally permit.'

There was a major difference, however, between Armstrong's study and my own. Although an outsider to the situation where he carried out his investigation, he had negotiated the opportunity to be involved in teaching, as well as observing, the children he studied. He could therefore appeal to the interplay between action and reflection, which is the usual basis for grounding the procedures of reflective practice and action research. The legitimacy of my own study would have to be established with reference to the reflective processes alone. The question was how this was to be achieved, if not by means of the usual claims to methodological soundness associated with the use of traditional research methods and techniques.

I did not at first see any connection between these methodological issues and the particular questions about special needs support that the study had set out to address. The two became inextricably linked, however, as I attempted to come to terms with the confusion and uncertainty encountered in making sense of Annette's and Adrian's learning, already discussed in detail earlier in the book. As had happened in the research on collaborative learning, I initially explained the problems away, assuming that the confusions would eventually sort themselves out as more information became available and clearer patterns began to emerge. This, after all, was what was expected to happen in a research process. But once I started thinking about the implications of these problems for practice, I realized that they were raising questions of relevance not only to my agenda regarding practitioner methodology but also with respect to the substantive questions of the study itself. The two agendas became so intertwined that the idea of innovative thinking which eventually took shape embodied in effect an answer to both. Thinking about the consequences for children's learning in practice provided the means to resolve the methodological questions raised by the research; the means discovered to resolve the methodological issues were found *also* to create a powerful tool for developing new ideas in response to concerns about children's learning.

TEACHING EXPERTISE AND PRACTITIONER RESEARCH

In terms of the research agenda, innovative thinking is an account of how learning occurs through thinking, in the context of practice or research. It identifies the interpretive expertise of teaching which, in appropriate circumstances, can be used for the purposes of research and the in-built safeguards which allow us to have confidence in the soundness of new ideas emerging. I have argued that the five questioning moves which make up the framework for innovative thinking are strategies that teachers use in the course of their everyday work. The five moves explain how new understandings and ideas for the development of practice are generated from existing understandings, by opening up existing thinking to re-examination. The interplay between the different moves not only helps to move thinking on but also provides the in-built self-checking device that allows us to have confidence in our conclusions, while keeping our minds open to new possibilities.

The framework for innovative thinking also provides the means to answer concerns about subjectivity that need to be considered by all researchers. In order to avoid being subjective, teacher-reseachers often turn to research methods as a safer means of distancing themselves and their own biases from the processes of data collection and analysis. This view is indeed reinforced in the literature, which contains voluminous advice about how to build safeguards into these processes to protect them from 'contamination'. Strategies such as triangulation, where the same situation is viewed from a number of perspectives – say, by eliciting views of different participants or using data generated by different means – are used to help to ensure that interpretations have not simply been taken at face value, but have been examined from a variety of different points of view.

The trouble is that if we distrust our subjectivity and try to suppress it by various means, we also suppress the use of the very resources which are the source of our thinking power. Innovative thinking offers an alternative means of achieving critical distance from our immediate interpretations: by *using* our subjective resources rather than suppressing them. Instead of hold-

ing back from making interpretations, it encourages us to use our immediate interpretations – or existing understandings – as the raw material for further thinking. We go to work on our existing thinking, using all our existing
knowledge, understandings and resources, to probe what is left unexamined
within it and reach out for new understandings. What is achieved through
this means is not greater objectivity, so much as a more *rigorously examined* subjectivity.

The interplay between the different moves allows teachers to create for
themselves the kind of continual questioning of interpretations from different perspectives that various forms of triangulation attempt to achieve, but
in a way that is achievable independently, and in the course of ordinary practice, without recourse to additional resources or special techniques.
Discussion and collaboration with colleagues can also be a helpful way of
achieving this, but it is not a prerequisite for challenging existing interpretations.

This is an important argument, because the usual assumption is that practice cannot measure up to the demands for rigorous thinking required by
research. Yet, in my study, it was the demands – or rather the commitments
– of *practice* that helped me to establish the criteria for methodological
soundness that needed to apply in the case of the *research*. Thinking about
the consequences for children in practice, if some of the possibilities that
occurred to me were left unexplored, enabled me to work out what the necessary constituents were of the interpretive framework needed to ensure that
all relevant features of a situation had indeed been taken into account. I
could see that we would not be fulfilling our responsibilities towards children if our interpretations consistently failed to take into account one or
more aspects of the situation reflected in the five questioning moves, no matter how assiduous and well-intentioned our approach to our professional
work. Criteria for soundness of our analysis are set by our professional commitments for both practice and research. Practitioner research which involves
simply an application of the interpretive skills and resources of teaching generates procedures which are different from but, in their own way, as rigorous, critical and self-critical as the most exacting traditional research process.

INNOVATIVE THINKING AND REFLECTIVE PRACTICE

This account of professional thinking and its potential application in the context of practitioner research has much in common with the work of Donald
Schon (1983). His theory of reflective practice played an important role in
helping to reinforce my own conviction that the interpretive expertise implied
by innovative thinking is applicable in the context of ordinary practice. It
also provided one important source of reinforcement of the idea that the
reflective expertise of teaching could be a legitimate and sufficient resource
for research.

Schon's account makes a distinction between two types of thinking that
professional workers use in their everyday practice. 'Knowing-in-action' is
the spontaneous, intuitive expertise which we make use of automatically

most of the time, when nothing about the situation alerts us to the need to think more consciously and deliberately about what is happening. 'Reflection-in-action' is a more explicit, deliberate, *questioning* kind of thinking, that we do when something worries, surprises or puzzles us about a particular situation: 'When the phenomenon at hand eludes the ordinary categories of knowledge-in-practice . . . the practitioner may surface and criticise his initial understanding of the phenomenon, construct a new description of it, and test the new description by on-the-spot experiment' (Schon, 1983, p. 63).

From his account of reflective practice, Schon draws a view of research which has some interesting parallels with my own study. This version of practitioner research involves teachers in reflecting upon their work away from the immediate context of practice. It is concerned with slowing down the processes of reflection-in-action in various ways for various purposes. In some cases, this may mean creating 'virtual worlds', or '. . . contexts for experiment within which practitioners can suspend or control some of the everyday impediments to rigorous reflection-in-action' (ibid., p. 162).

The classrooms in which I carried out my investigation might be seen as providing me with my own 'virtual world': a particular kind of situation and experience which I would not necessarily have encountered in the normal course of events, and where I could develop my ideas unimpeded by expectations of having to fulfil a particular professional role within it. Although the absence of a teaching role put me at a disadvantage in some respects, it also allowed me to slow down the interpretive processes which precede decisions to act, to examine them more closely and reflect upon their implications not just for the reflective process generally but also for the task of pursuing concerns about children's learning.

However, although Schon's work provided an important support for the development of my own thinking at numerous points during the study, my account of innovative thinking differs from Schon's theory of reflective practice in a number of ways. First, Schon was not concerned with analysing the thinking of teachers in particular. He was working at a more general level, trying to develop a theory of reflection extrapolated from accounts of professional practice in many different areas. The framework for innovative thinking that I have described is derived from and adapted to the specific context of classroom and school. It also introduces the idea of an in-built self-checking process, created through the interplay between the five questioning moves, which is not part of Schon's account of reflective practice generally.

There is also little reference in Schon's work to how practitioners incorporate the ideas of others into the reflective process. His account makes the practitioner sound almost self-sufficient, as if new knowledge emerges from reflection alone without recourse to the ideas of others. In my account, on the other hand, external ideas are incorporated into the reflective process not as ready-made solutions but to support the functioning of the five moves. I have argued that there is a vast resource of material to draw on, for instance, to extend the range of connections that we are able to make between school and classroom processes and individual responses, to help us to recognize alternative ways of 'seeing' what is happening in our classrooms by bringing different norms of good learning to bear. Confidence in the soundness of our understandings does not depend upon extensive knowledge and use of the literature, since no interpretation can ever be exhaustive. Nevertheless, the more resources we have available, the more complex the analysis we will be able to aspire to achieve, and the more possibilities we will be able to generate for supporting and enhancing children's learning.

Moreover, Schon speaks of practitioners constructing a 'theory of the unique case' in a response to a problematic situation. This might be taken to imply that the outcomes have relevance only to that one situation or individual child. My studies of Annette's and Adrian's learning, on the other hand, led to insights that were generalizable as well as individual-specific. Innovative thinking generates new ideas and possibilities for the development of practice which have an impact beyond the immediate situation, influencing our thinking and work with children more generally.

Where difficulties in learning are discussed, Schon tends to treat them rather unproblematically as direct products of teachers' own individual thinking and practice. A 'failure' to learn on the part of the child is treated as symptomatic of a defect in the teacher's 'own instruction' (ibid., p. 66), reconstructing unhelpfully the child's failure as the teacher's failure. I have argued, on the other hand, that the dynamics which shape children's responses to school experience and the sense that we make of their responses are far too complex to be seen in individual-deficit terms, whether deficits are attributed to individual teachers or individual learners.

Lastly, no account seems to be taken, in Schon's work, of the impact of ideology upon thinking. A teacher who interprets a child's failure to learn as a deficiency of the child is seen as individually lacking in 'art' rather than giving expression to her concerns about children's learning through the most pervasive and persuasive of prevailing discourses. Schon recognizes the possibility that, for various reasons, the interpretive system may close off and render itself 'immune to reflection'. However, this is seen more as a localized problem of particular individuals and institutional circumstances, rather than a wider pattern associated with culturally available systems of thought and value internalized by individuals. Innovative thinking, on the other hand, links up the reflective process to its wider social and political context. It helps to ensure that *concerns about* individuals are not construed as *problems of* individuals, by generating a process which leads us to review routinely and systematically possibilities for understanding children's responses to school learning other than as a reflection of personal characteristics and biographical limitations.

THE CUTTING EDGE

Innovative thinking, then, is more that just an approach to the task of pursuing concerns about children's learning. It is also a theory of professional reflection and learning which makes explicit the basis for developing a legitimate mode of practitioner research derived from the interpretive expertise of teaching. Innovative thinking offers a methodology for research which seeks to capitalize on teachers' existing interpretive resources and skills and so maximize their powers of thinking and learning from and through research. To foster it, INSET providers need to ensure that practitioners have opportunities not only to become acquainted with research methodology, but also recognize the power of their existing resources to generate sound new understandings of children's learning. We need to create opportunities which will allow teachers to strengthen and increase their existing powers, and extend the knowledge base upon which they currently draw to stimulate thinking.

The stories illustrate how much could be learnt if teachers had more time and opportunity to observe and reflect in a sustained way on children's learning, and to engage in classroom research. In Chapter 5, I examined in detail the new areas of thinking and further enquiry that were opened up for me by my study of these two children's learning, showing how pursuing these could not only benefit the individual concerned but also benefit our work with children generally. These outcomes were not simply tied to the teaching and learning of writing, but opened up more general questions relating to teaching, learning and assessment. Funding for practitioner research needs to be made available to allow teachers to pursue *on their own behalf* questions arising from their practice that cannot readily, or most effectively, be pursued under the ordinary circumstances of practice. Teachers also need to be commissioned on our *collective behalf* to carry out research which will increase our collective understanding of the dynamics of learning and teaching, which other teachers can use to resource, stimulate and enrich their own thinking.

Unfortunately, many of the steps currently being taken to foster school improvement and improved standards of achievement make *shortcomings* of existing practice the focus for development. This, coupled with a climate of accountability and competitiveness between schools, risks creating a widespread reaction of defensiveness and dependence on external evaluation as a stimulus for development and change. This directly undermines the approach to professional thinking and learning which underpins the ideas proposed in this book.

If the aim is to enhance the quality of learning and achievement in schools, this will best be fostered by an approach to professional development which is duly respectful of the complexities of the teacher's task, and is designed to recognize, nurture and strengthen the expertise within. I have shown that the task of pursuing concerns about children's learning can, if approached through innovative thinking, provide the cutting edge for the development of our thinking. The strong sense of responsibility which we feel towards children whose learning concerns us prompts the thinking that leads on to new understanding. It provides a continual resource for teachers' professional learning and, if we allow it to, a constant stimulus to the development of education generally.

Bibliography

Abercrombie, M. L. J. (1960) *The Anatomy of judgement*, Penguin, Harmondsworth.

Ainscow, M. (ed.) (1991) *Effective schools for all*, David Fulton, London.

Ainscow, M. and Tweddle, D. (1988) *Encouraging classroom success*, David Fulton, London.

Applebee, A. N. (1978) *The child's concept of story*, University of Chicago Press, Chicago.

Armstrong, M. (1980) *Closely observed children: The diary of a primary classroom*, Writers and Readers Cooperative, Oxford.

Armstrong, M. (1981) Louise and the case of painting, in J. Nixon, (ed.) *A teacher's guide to action research*, Grant McIntyre, London.

Armstrong, M. (1990) Another way of looking, *Forum* Vol. 33, no. 1, pp. 12–16.

Bell, P. and Best, R. (1986) *Supportive education*, Blackwell, Oxford.

Booth, T., Potts, P. and Swann, W. (eds.) (1987) *Preventing difficulties in learning: Curricula for all*, Blackwell, Oxford.

Booth, T., Swann, W., Masterton, M. and Potts, P. (eds.) (1992) *Curricula for diversity in education*, Routledge, London.

Calkins, L. M. (1983) *Lessons from a child: On the teaching and learning of writing*, Heinemann, Portsmouth, New Hampshire.

Calkins, L. M. (1986) *The art of teaching writing*, Heinemann, Portsmouth, New Hampshire.

Calkins, L. M. (1991) *Living between the lines*, Heinemann, Portsmouth, New Hampshire.

Christie, F. (ed.) (1990) *Literacy for a changing world*, Australian Council for Educational Research, Victoria.

Clough, P. (1988) Bridging 'mainstream' and 'special' education: a curriculum problem, *Journal of Curriculum Studies*, Vol. 20, no. 4, pp. 327–38.

Crichton, M. (1991) *Jurassic Park*, Arrow, London.

Davies, B. (1989) *Frogs and snails and feminist tales: Pre-school children and gender*, Allen & Unwin, Sydney.

Department for Education (1994) *The Code of Practice on the identification and assessment of special educational needs*, Central Office of Information, London.

Department of Education and Science (1978) *Special educational needs*: Report of the committee of enquiry into the education of handicapped children and young people, HMSO, London.

Donaldson, M. (1978) *Children's Minds*, Fontana, London.

Drummond, M. J. (1993) *Assessing children's learning*, David Fulton, London.

Dyson, A. (1990) Special educational needs and the concept of change, *Oxford Review of Education*, Vol. 16, no. 1, pp. 55–6.

Dyson, A. and Gains, C. W. (1993) (eds.) *Rethinking special needs in mainstream schools: towards the year 2000*, David Fulton, London.

Eagleton, T. (1983) *Literary theory: an introduction*, Basil Blackwell, Oxford.

Easen, P. (1987) All at sixes and sevens, in T. Booth, P. Potts and W. Swann (eds.) *Preventing difficulties in learning*, Blackwell, Oxford.

Elliott, J. (1991) *Action research for educational change*, Open University Press, Milton Keynes.

Fox, C. (1993) *At the very edge of the forest: the influence of literature on story telling by children*, Cassell, London.

Goldstein, H. and Noss, R. (1990) Against the stream, *Forum*, Vol. 33, no. 1, pp. 4–6.

Graves, D. (1983) *Writing: Teachers and children at work*, Heinemann, Portsmouth, New Hampshire.

Graves, D. (1984) *A Researcher learns to write: Selected articles and monographs*, Heinemann, London.

Graves, D. (1989) *Experiment with fiction*, Heinemann, Portsmouth, New Hampshire.

Gregory, E. (1993a) Reading between the lines, *Times Educational Supplement*, 15 October.

Gregory, E. (1993b) Sweet and sour: Learning to read in a British and Chinese school, *English in Education*, Vol. 27, no. 3, pp. 53–9.

Harste, J. C., Woodward, V. A. and Burke, C. L. (1984) *Language stories and literacy lessons*, Heinemann, Portsmouth, New Hampshire.

Hart, S. (1986a) Evaluating support teaching, *Gnosis 9*, ILEA, pp. 26-29.

Hart, S. (1986b) In-class support teaching: Tackling Fish, *British Journal of Special Education*, Vol. 13, no. 2, pp. 57–8.

Hart, S. (1987) A lesson from Humanities, in T. Booth, P. Potts and W. Swann (eds.) *Preventing difficulties in learning: Curricula for all*, Blackwell, Oxford.

Hart, S. (1989a) Everest in Plimsolls, in D. Mongon and S. Hart (eds.) *Improving classroom behaviour: new directions for teachers and pupils*, Cassell, London.

Hart, S. (1989b) *Collaborative learning, group work and the spaces in between*, paper presented at conference of British Educational Research Association, London, September 1989.

Hart, S. (1992a) Differentiation: Way forward or retreat?, *British Journal of Special Education*, Vol. 19, no. 1, pp. 10–12.

Hart, S. (1992b) Differentiation: Part of the problem or part of the solution?, *The Curriculum Journal*, Vol. 3, no. 2, pp. 131–42.

Hart, S. (1992c) Collaborative classrooms, in T. Booth, W. Swann, M. Masterton and P. Potts (eds.) *Curricula for diversity in education: Learning for All*, Routledge, London.

Hart, S. (1994) *The innovative practitioner: reconceptualising the special needs task*, PhD thesis, University of Greenwich

Heath, S. B. (1983) *Ways with words: Language, life and work in communities and classrooms*, Cambridge University Press.

Holbrook, D. (1964) *English for the rejected: training literacy in the lower streams of the secondary school*, Cambridge University Press.

Holt, J. (1969) *How children fail*, Penguin, Harmondsworth.

Hornsey, A. W. (1972) A foreign language for all?, in *Centre for Information on Language teaching Reports and Papers 8, Teaching modern languages across the ability range*, CILT, London.

Kress, G. (1982) *Learning to write*, Routledge & Kegan Paul, London.

Littlefair, A. (1993) Let's be positive about genre, *Reading*, Vol. 26, no. 3, pp. 2–6.

Lunzer, E. and Gardner, K. (eds.) (1979) *The effective use of reading*, Heinemann, London.

McCall, G. J. and Simmons, J. L. (eds.) (1969) *Issues in participant observation: A text and reader*, Addison-Wesley, London.

McNiff, J. (1988) *Action Research: principles and practice*, Macmillan, London.

Miles, T. R. and Miles, E. (1983) *Help for dyslexic children*, Methuen, London.

Mongon, D. and Hart, S. with Ace, C. and Rawlings, A. (1989) *Improving Classroom Behaviour: New Directions for Teachers and Pupils*, Cassell, London.

National Commission on Education (1993) *Learning to succeed: A radical look at education today and a strategy for the future*, Report of the Paul Hamlyn Foundation, Heinemann, London.

Protherough, R. (1983) *Encouraging writing*, Methuen, London.

Pumfrey. P, and Reason. R, (1992) *Specific learning difficulties (dyslexia): Challenges and responses*, NFER-Routledge, London.

Pye, J. (1988) *Invisible children: Who are the real losers at school?*, Oxford University Press.

Rosen, H. (1992) The politics of writing, in K. Kimberley, M. Meek, J. Miller, (eds.) *New readings: Contributions to an understanding of literacy*, A. C. Black, London.

Rowland S. (1984) *The enquiring classroom*, Falmer, Lewes.

Rowland, S. (1986) Classroom enquiry: An approach to understanding children, in D. Hustler, A. Cassidy and E. C. Cuff (eds.) *Action research in classrooms and schools*, Allen & Unwin, London.

Salzberger-Wittenberg, I., Henry, G. and Osborne, E. (1983) *The emotional experience of learning and teaching*, Routledge & Kegan Paul, London.

Schon, D. A. (1983) *The reflective practitioner: How professionals think in action*, Basic Books, New York.

Selden, R. (1985) *A reader's guide to contemporary literary theory*, Harvester Press, Brighton.

Smith, F. (1983) Reading like a writer, *Language Arts*, Vol. 60, no. 5, pp. 558–67.

Snowling, M. J. (1985) *Children's written language difficulties*, NFER Nelson, Windsor.

Snowling, M. J. (1987) *Dyslexia: A cognitive developmental perspective*, Blackwell, Oxford.

Steedman, C. (1982) *The tidy house: Little girls writing*, Virago, London.

Stenhouse, L. (1975) *An introduction to curriculum research and development*, Heinemann, London.

Temple, C. A., Nathan, R. G. and Burris, N. A. (1982) *The beginnings of writing: A practical guide to a young child's discovery of writing through the scribbling, spelling and composing stages*, Allyn & Bacon, Boston, Mass.

Thomas, G. and Feiler, A. (1988) *Planning special needs*, Blackwell, Oxford.

Tizard, B. and Hughes, M. (1985) *Young children learning: Talking and thinking at home and at school*, Fontana, London.

Turner, M. (1990) *Sponsored reading failure: an object lesson*, The Education Unit, Warlingham.

Volosinov, V. N. (1973) *Marxism and the philosophy of language*, Harvard University Press.

Vygotsky, L. S. (1962) *Thought and language*, MIT Press, Cambridge Mass.

Wells, G. (1987) *The meaning makers: Children learning language and and using language to learn*, Hodder & Stoughton, London.

Willinsky, J. (1990) *The new literacy: Redefining reading and writing in schools*,

Routledge, New York.

Winter, R. (1989) *Learning from experience: Principles and practice in action-research* Falmer, Lewes.

Young, C. and Robinson, E. (1987) Reading/writing in the culture of the classroom, in B. Corcoran, and E. Evans, (eds.) *Readers, texts, teachers*, Open University Press, Milton Keynes.

Index